Southern Literary Studies

LOUIS D. RUBIN, JR., EDITOR

**The Poetry Reviews of
ALLEN TATE
1924–1944**

The Poetry Reviews of ALLEN TATE 1924–1944

Edited, with an Introduction,
by Ashley Brown
and Frances Neel Cheney

Louisiana State University Press
Baton Rouge and London

Designer: Albert Crochet
Typeface: Linotron Trump Medieval
Typesetter: Graphic Composition, Inc.
Printer and binder: Thomson-Shore, Inc.

LIBRARY OF CONGRESS CATALOGING IN PUBLICATION DATA

Tate, Allen, 1899–
    The poetry reviews of Allen Tate, 1924–1944.
    (Southern literary studies)
    1. American Poetry—20th century—Book reviews.
2. English poetry—20th century—Book reviews.
I. Brown, Ashley, 1934–   II. Cheney, Frances
Neel, 1906–   III. Title. IV. Series.
PS324.T25   1983   821'.52'09   82–12687
ISBN 0–8071–1057–4

The Introduction first appeared under the title "Allen Tate:
A Poet on Poetry, 1924–1944" in the November 1979 issue of
Poetry. Reprinted by permission.

The photograph of Allen Tate (1930) appears through the courtesy of
Helen H. Tate.

Contents

Preface

THIS VOLUME is a chronicle of modern poetry from 1924 to
1944. During those two decades Allen Tate was extremely active as an essayist and reviewer; reviewing books was probably his
main source of income when he was a young man. He also reviewed
fiction, philosophy, and Civil War history, but his central concern
was the poetry written by his contemporaries, who in many cases
were also friends. In this collection we can see him judging and
helping to create the reputations of a dozen poets; he returns to
some of them three or four times. This collection is thus a fairly
important commentary on one phase of our literary history, and it
complements Allen Tate's *Essays of Four Decades* and *Memories
and Opinions*. We talked to him about this book several times before his death in February, 1979. He was very enthusiastic about it
and indeed made a number of suggestions. The pieces on Pound's
early *Cantos*, Eliot's *Ash Wednesday*, Robinson's *Talifer*, and
MacLeish's *Conquistador* have been reprinted in some of Tate's collections of essays, including *Essays of Four Decades*; but they were
originally reviews, and he liked the idea of their being presented
again in this new context. A few other pieces, such as the reviews
of Cummings' *Viva* and Edna St. Vincent Millay's *Fatal Interview*,
were actually collected in *Reactionary Essays on Poetry and Ideas*
(1936) and then allowed to go out of print. The long omnibus review
that came out in the *Southern Review* in 1937 was included in *Reason in Madness* (1941).

Allen Tate seems to have been fortunate in his editors at every
stage of his reviewing. His Fugitive friend Donald Davidson was the
literary editor of the Nashville *Tennessean* during the 1920s, and

this is where he made his début as critic; in 1924 he contributed twenty-nine reviews to Davidson's weekly book page. By the end of that year he was living in New York, where he became a friend of Edmund Wilson of *The New Republic* and Mark Van Doren of *The Nation*. These two journals of opinion were the chief outlets for his criticism for several years. Then the famous quarterlies, beginning with *Hound and Horn*, gave him more space, and the reviewer gradually became the essayist. By the early 1940s Tate was himself an editor when he took over the *Sewanee Review* for two years. After that period his reviews were infrequent, and so it seems proper to end this collection at 1944.

A.B.
F.N.C.

**The Poetry Reviews of
ALLEN TATE
1924–1944**

Introduction

WHEN ALLEN TATE started writing reviews in 1924, modernist poetry, mostly brought out in London during the preceding decade, had recently found its true home in the United States; but there were few critics who were prepared to deal with it as incisively as Pound had done. The established critics of the period, Mencken and Van Wyck Brooks, usually treated poetry as a minor issue when they looked at it at all, and Edmund Wilson from the beginning felt more at ease with novelists. After 1922, when *The Waste Land* was published more or less simultaneously in London and New York, it was possible for an American poet to make his way without going abroad; and the small flood of important books that started coming out in 1923—*Harmonium, Tulips and Chimneys, Observations, Chills and Fever*, and the others—presented a challenge. It was under these circumstances that Tate quickly came to the fore as a reviewer. He easily made the transition from the Nashville of the Fugitives to the New York of Hart Crane and Cummings, but he never surrendered his first set of loyalties. His southerner's sense of place and region was in some ways an advantage: it could allow him to respect other people's regions as much as his own. (See, for instance, his review of Malcolm Cowley's *Blue Juniata* in 1929.) The South has never "produced" many poets or critics to this day (most of the talent still goes into fiction writing), and a southerner may well stand in awe of a poetry center like Harvard.

Tate, however, was absolutely assured about his opinions, partly, I think, because of his classical and philosophical training at Vanderbilt. He had the long view of history, and in the dozens of reviews that he wrote during the 1920s and 1930s he always, despite his frequent enthusiasm for a new book, referred the individual case to

1

a set of standards that he had firmly developed while he was a student. Thus he made this judgment about the poetry of Sacheverell and Osbert Sitwell in 1925—a judgment that stands up very well after half a century:

> The properties of decoration were exploited by the French seventeenth century and the English eighteenth. There is much of it in Pope. But there is very little of it in the Romantic poetry of any age; for it thrives only in a society emotionally unambitious, in which an imaginative conquest of a universe is less important than immediate social relations and allegiances. The decay of the Romantic movement has delivered poets into a world rather tired emotionally, suspicious of the Romantic preoccupation with a doubtful Infinite. And they are deprived of capacity for the kind of allegiance that enabled Pope, who knew a rascal when he saw one, to write sympathetically of Villiers because Villiers stood for the foundation of his society—Church and State.... The Sitwell brothers, interesting enough as expert craftsmen in minor modes, are producing mostly decoration and lack direction entirely. They are neo-classical sensibilities without a milieu.

"The decay of the Romantic movement" or some such phrase occurs quite frequently in Tate's criticism. This is of course part of a large historical view. He early arrived at the conclusion that a modern poet can seldom if ever realize a complete action in his work; historical circumstances make it almost impossible. This conviction underlies his celebrated review of Crane's *The Bridge* in 1930. But I don't think that it was altogether a matter of philosophical conviction. Tate was a poet before he was a critic, and his poet's instinct somehow made him suspicious of the large "epical" performance. The recently published literary correspondence between Tate and his Fugitive friend Donald Davidson is very useful in assessing his attitude, especially during the 1920s. At that time—to be precise, in the year 1926—Davidson was writing an ambitious long poem called *The Tall Men*, which in certain passages resembles *The Bridge*; Tate knew both poems at almost every stage of their composition. He remarked to Davidson, "I am convinced that Milton himself could not write a Paradise Lost now. Minds are less important for literature than cultures; our minds are as good as they ever were, but our culture is dissolving." Then at the end of that year he wrote the first version of "Ode to the Confederate Dead."

We can now tell from the published correspondence that its germ was the passage about the charge of the Confederate infantry. (Tate told me in 1958, as we were strolling over part of the battlefield at Gettysburg, that the lines about "the inscrutable infantry rising/ Demons out of the earth" came from the account of the battle in *Harper's Weekly*.) The temptation to write a large "heroic" poem, as his two friends were doing, indeed to compete with them, must have been considerable at this point. But the poem as we have had it all along is a meditation in which the heroism is checked. As Elizabeth Bishop, a poet of a rather different sort, has said, "Something needn't be large to be good."

Tate nevertheless was obsessed by the long poem, and he took up this theme in reviews of major works by Robinson, Pound, Aiken, Crane, and MacLeish. Of Robinson, whom he placed first among living poets in 1924, he said:

> In his long poems he merely presents series after series of abstruse and perhaps exact analyses of successive mental states. His people never act, never do anything; they only think, feel, suffer; and the things in the outer world that make them suffer are utterly left out in his report of them; they are just so many abstracted minds. . . . In Mr. Robinson there is no drama; there is no action that draws his men and women into a unity.

Robinson, despite the great respect that Tate had for him, was perhaps old-fashioned in his narrative technique. That couldn't be said of Tate's contemporary MacLeish, whose *Conquistador* used to be the most widely admired poem of its generation. The narrator, Bernal, is a modern personality not unlike the narrators in Hemingway's early novels. But, said Tate, "There is not one moment of action objectively rendered in the whole poem. There is constantly and solely the pattern of sensation that surrounds the moment of action. The technique for rendering this quality is MacLeish's contribution to poetic style, and he has so perfected it that later poets will touch it at the peril of the most slavish imitation."

In some respects Pound was the most successful poet of his time for Tate, precisely because he avoided the semblance of an action; at least this was true in 1931, when Tate reviewed *A Draft of XXX Cantos* at length:

The secret of his form is this: conversation. The cantos are talk, talk, talk; not by any one in particular to any one else in particular; they are just rambling talk. At least each canto is a cunningly devised imitation of a polite conversation, in which no one presses any subject very far. The length of breath, the span of conversational energy, is the length of the canto. The conversationalist pauses; there is just enough left hanging in the air to give him a new start; so that the transitions between the cantos are natural and easy.

But Tate's enthusiasm for the *Cantos* didn't last beyond the first thirty; *Cantos LII–LXXI*, which he reviewed in 1941, left him "very, very cold" because he could no longer "attribute structure" to the verse: "Between John Adams and the agrarian emperors of China there is only a community of economic abstraction, which Major Douglas alone understands today, and of high courtesy, which Mr. Pound evidently despairs of reviving." I think, however, that Tate's marvelous description of *A Draft of XXX Cantos* as conversation will survive as one of the ways of getting at the poem; there is really no settled way of reading it.

Tate's heroes among poets included Dante, Baudelaire, Yeats, and Eliot, in somewhat that order. (Sooner or later he paid tribute to each of them in his own poetry.) In 1927, when he was reviewing *Trinc* by Phelps Putnam, a poet whom he continued to admire, he quoted a passage from "Bill and *Les Enfants Pendus*," and then he remarked:

> To match the effect of this passage, one could go to the *Divine Comedy*; it has something of the shock of the question that Guido Cavalcanti's father asks Dante, out of the depths of his flaming coffin:
>
> > Di subito drizzato gridò: Come
> > Dicesti: egli ebbe? non viv' egli ancora?
> > *No fiere gli occhi suoi lo dolce lome?*
>
> The ingenuity, however, with which Mr. Putnam prepares for these surprises of contrast, results more often in a *nouveau frisson* not unlike that sought after so diligently by the French Romantics. Putnam's lines
>
> > In Springfield, Massachusetts, I devoured
> > The mystic, the improbable, the Rose—
>
> are, of course, much nearer Baudelaire than to anything in Dante. The typical instance of the romantic "shudder" is Baudelaire's sudden tran-

sition, in "Femmes Damnées," from an impersonal description of perverted sensuality to a dire, equally impersonal vision of its consequences:

Descendez, descendez, lamentables victimes,
Descendez le chemin de l'enfer éternel.

Putnam, a New England Romantic who, for Tate, embodied certain regional characteristics, is thus placed within a large historical context; he becomes a *kind* of modern Baudelaire. The lines from "Femmes Damnées" must have been a touchstone for Tate, because he continued to refer to them in reviews of translations by Aldous Huxley (1932) and Edna Millay and George Dillon (1936).

Putnam, an unjustly neglected poet nowadays, was only one of the Americans whom Tate promoted in his criticism. The others would include Crane (whom he placed first), Cummings, MacLeish, Cowley, Léonie Adams and Louise Bogan, John Peale Bishop, Mark Van Doren, and the young Yvor Winters. Indeed, he reviewed most of them two or three times, and in his essay on "American Poetry Since 1920," which he wrote near the end of that decade, nearly all of them appear prominently with their elders like Stevens and Marianne Moore. I think that he was at his best with these poets of his generation, perhaps because he was the first to review them in most cases; there were no received opinions about them, and he had a free hand, as it were. I have put Léonie Adams and Louise Bogan together in this list because Tate almost invariably did so, as in "American Poetry Since 1920":

Miss Bogan's *Body of This Death* (1923), a slight but almost perfect exhibit, announced the most accomplished woman poet of the time; Miss Bogan had reduced a sharp sense of peripheral sensations, to which women are peculiarly sensitive, to form. But Miss Adams's *Those Not Elect* (1925) heralded a close rival. Miss Adams's range is, in fact, considerably greater than Miss Bogan's, and her style is richer and more mature; her mind is probably the freest in contemporary poetry; it is susceptible to release by all the experience at her command. Her style is a little too heavily burdened with a superabundance of imagery; and her poems often conceal their central ideas; this defect of composition may be corrected in time.

It is arguable that Tate, by putting Miss Bogan and Miss Adams in tandem, did them a disservice—as he said, they are quite unlike each other—but he undoubtedly advanced their reputations, all the way to the Bollingen Prize which they eventually shared. Of the poets in this group, Winters had the farthest to go in 1927; he was the one who would write his best poetry in a rather different style a decade or so later. But in 1927 Tate said of *The Bare Hills*: "This book, had it appeared ten years ago, would have won its author the first place among the Imagist poets." Winters, incidentally, must be Tate's closest rival as a reviewer during this period, and in fact he frequently discussed the same poets: Robinson, MacLeish, Stevens, Crane, Louise Bogan, and Léonie Adams (separately); and Winters in his turn reviewed Tate in 1932. (Somebody should write a book that traces the relationship between Tate's group in Tennessee and the Gyroscope group in California; there are many points of comparison.)

In retrospect it might seem that Tate was somewhat slow in recognizing the importance of Wallace Stevens; the first major critical presentation of Stevens came with R. P. Blackmur's essay of 1932, after the second *Harmonium*. Winters said in 1922, before the first *Harmonium*, that "A pigeon's wing may make as great an image as a man's tragedy, and in the poetry of Mr. Wallace Stevens has done so." Stevens, for various reasons, political and otherwise, was late in coming into his great fame, and even in 1944, when Tate asserted that "there can be little doubt that Stevens and Eliot are the most impressive poets in the modern movement in English," this opinion would have been considered extreme. His early review of *Harmonium* juxtaposed with Edith Sitwell's *Bucolic Comedies* (perhaps the reviewer's lot of books for the week) is still of some interest, however, because it points back to the dandyism that is really present in the Stevens of *Harmonium* and that tends to be slighted in the Age of Bloom.

By the early 1940s Tate was nearing the end of his reviewing days, and the title of his piece on Horace Gregory, Cummings, Pound, and *Five Young American Poets* (including Jarrell and Berryman) was "The Last Omnibus." But he generously, even eagerly took up the cause of another generation that included Delmore Schwartz, Karl Shapiro, and Robert Lowell. His review of Shapiro's *Person, Place, and Thing* in 1943 was extraordinary—a public letter to the poet:

> Your poetry moves me because it has, for the first time since T. S. Eliot's
> arrival more than twenty-five years ago, that final honesty which is rare,

unpleasant, and indispensable in a poet of our time. I envy you because, having striven for this quality, I have failed; I have never, in any poem, been able *to get it all down*. You very nearly do get it all down, at moments wholly. I address you from a past remotely different from yours, from a radically different conception of the history and destiny of this country of ours; yet if you will allow me the sentiment, the common humanity of poets is not founded in sympathy of views or of politics, but in that special savagery of attack which they must acknowledge across all barriers, as I wish at this moment to acknowledge in your poems.

This eloquent statement no doubt says more about Tate and his poetry than it does about Shapiro; but that is as it should be.

As for Tate's introduction to Lowell's *Land of Unlikeness* in the following year, that was even more remarkable in its way than his foreword to Crane's *White Buildings* in 1926. Lowell was almost unknown in 1944, whereas Crane was at the center of a brilliant literary generation in New York when *White Buildings* came out. In two sentences Tate already suggested what the course of Lowell's career was to be:

On the one hand, the Christian symbolism is intellectualized and frequently given a savage satirical direction; it points to the disappearance of the Christian experience from the modern world, and stands, perhaps, for the poet's own effort to recover it. On the other hand, certain shorter poems, like "A Suicidal Nightmare" and "Death from Cancer," are richer in immediate experience than the explicitly religious poems; they are more dramatic, the references being personal and historical and the symbolism less willed and explicit.

Lowell was probably the last important poet whom Tate "discovered," though he frequently went out of his way to assist still younger poets. But after 1944 he wrote only a handful of reviews of any kind. (His typical critical performance would henceforth be a lecture reprinted as an essay.) In another year or so his successor, Randall Jarrell, moved from Nashville to New York to be literary editor of *The Nation*, and the postwar era was underway. American literary culture was undoubtedly set at a higher level than it had been in 1924, and much of the credit must go to Tate. That is a matter of record.

Ashley Brown

Edna St. Vincent Millay, Edith Sitwell, Wallace Stevens

The Harp-Weaver and Other Poems, by Edna St. Vincent Millay. Harper and Brothers, 1923.
Bucolic Comedies, by Edith Sitwell. Duckworth Company (London), 1923.
Harmonium, by Wallace Stevens. Alfred A. Knopf, 1923.

EDNA ST. VINCENT MILLAY still sits comfortably in the foremost place among the lyric poets of this country. *The Harp-Weaver and Other Poems* comes out now as the fourth book of poetry from the hand of Miss Millay; and it is apparent that the fine promise of *Renascence* and of most of the work in *Second April* is indeed growing into so even and consistent a performance that she can just about stand the ultimate test of a poet's inspiration—the test of quantity. Certainly Mrs. Wylie and Miss Louise Bogan, despite the cameo-like perfection of the one and the vivid power of the other, can make no such demonstration. I can think of only three other American poets who could offer the double claim of bulk and quality—Robinson, Sandburg and Frost; but they are different; all that they share with Miss Millay or each other is a common excellence.

Perhaps in this volume Miss Millay does little more than sustain her reputation. The title-poem, which won the Pulitzer prize for 1922, is only less a tour de force than the well-known "Blue Flower in the Bog," and is as disappointing as most prize poems; its effects but ill conceal the deliberation back of them; the simplicity of statement is too arduously won. Turning to Part Two, we at once suspect the origin of this very wise simplicity, A. E. Housman; indeed, "The Betrothal" seems hardly Miss Millay's. So it is to the two sonnet-sequences that we must go for the best work in the volume. For depth of insight and mastery of technique Miss Millay's "Sonnets," the love-and-beauty series, surpasses the more sacred "Sonnets from the Portuguese":

> Lord Archer, Death, whom sent you in your stead?
> What faltering prentice fumbled at your bow,
> That now should wander with the insanguine dead
> In whom forever the bright blood must flow?
> Or is it rather that impairing Time
> Renders yourself so random, or so dim?
> Or are you sick of shadows and would climb
> A while to light, a while detaining him?
> For know, this was no mortal youth, to be
> Of you confounded, but a heavenly guest,
> Assuming earthly garb for love of me,
> And hell's demure attire for love of jest:
> Bringing me asphodel and a dark feather,
> He will return, and we shall laugh together!

"Sonnets from an Ungrafted Tree" discover the beautiful in a loveless marriage—the tragic beauty of desolation and dead illusion, like that of which Mr. Robinson writes in his "The Unforgiven," only Miss Millay offers the natural solution of death. Here, Miss Millay makes complete use of her sharp awareness of the significant in the superficially trivial incidents of human intercourse, and it is the sustained austerity, in her attitude of sympathy and irony, which places these sonnets, along with certain others in previous books, among the best in the language.

In "Sonnets from an Ungrafted Tree" there is a new technical device: every sonnet ends with a seven-stress line, with a peculiarly lingering rhythm, but it is impossible to say whether this innovation is a permanent contribution to the sonnet-form.

If Edna St. Vincent Millay is the most accomplished woman lyricist in America, then Edith Sitwell is easily the most striking figure in contemporary poetry in England. She is the leader of the famous "Wheels" group, so cordially despised by the Georgians; her brothers are Osbert and Sacheverell Sitwell, who are barely less competent than she; and to this group, in a way, belong also Aldous Huxley and, as an influence, T. S. Eliot—a movement of radical tendency in poetry whose achievement is yet to be established.

But Miss Sitwell's importance is beyond dispute; she is both of and above her school. She is not a lyric poet, as Miss Millay is a lyric poet; perhaps, without her intense emotional equipment, she could have been a mathematician; as we see her, she is an emotional cerebralist. A hasty glance through *Bucolic Comedies* is rewarded with an impression of the most elaborate artificiality; but there is more than that. Behind the almost strutting imagery and the eccentric versification—both are woven into a flawless pattern—is a guiding perception that can be explained only in terms of a unique and distinguished mind; like Aubrey Beardsley, she creates a new world with a law of its own, a world of sugary, mawkish brutality and the subtlest caricature. She is rather French than English and obviously draws on the late Parnassians and Decadents for her variety of forms and mixed vocabulary which reminds one of Baudelaire. For the rare and precise word, Miss Sitwell puts Wilde and the precious 'Nineties to shame:

> "Madame Myrrhine, if you please,"
> Fawning said the barber breeze,
> "I will coif as light as air
> That Arabian wind your hair."
> See
> The tall Spanish jade
> With hair black as nightshade
> Worn as a cockade!
> Flee her eyes' gasconade
> And her gown's parade
> (As stiff as a brigade).

E. E. Cummings, Wallace Stevens, and William Carlos Williams are the foremost "radicals" in America, and they probably rank in the order named; they are the American counterpart of "Wheels." But where Miss Sitwell often indulges in a bewildering "fine excess" Mr. Stevens' exacting sense of verbal economy limits him to a few vivid and significant strokes, and his poem is done:

THE CURTAINS IN THE HOUSE OF THE METAPHYSICIAN

> It comes about that the drifting of these curtains
> Is full of long motions; as the ponderous
> Deflations of distance; or as clouds
> Inseparable from their afternoons;

> Or the changing of light, the dropping
> Of the silence, wide sleep and solitude
> Of night, in which all motion
> Is beyond us, as the firmament,
> Up-rising and down-falling, bares
> The last largeness, bold to see.

Or this:

> What syllable are you seeking,
> Vocalissimus,
> In the distances of sleep?
> Speak it.

Like the Elizabethans, these poets are after new meanings for old words—a new vocabulary for a completely individual expression. Mr. Stevens is an intellectualist; a tree of itself is meaningless to him:

> But, after all, I know a tree that bears
> A semblance to the thing I have in mind.

Wallace Stevens is an explorer of the exotic; his diction, in strangeness of effect, lags but little after Miss Sitwell. His better poems present a freshness of observation; the trite phrase is entirely absent from his work.

From the Nashville *Tennessean* (February 10, 1924)

E. E. Cummings

Tulips and Chimneys, by E. E. Cummings. Thomas Seltzer, 1923.

IT'S GOING TO BE very much like playing Leo Ornstein on an accordian to try to render a just account of E. E. Cummings' first volume of poetry in terms of a popular review. But so splendid, so important, to my mind is Mr. Cummings' verse that I am very willing to suffer the results of inconclusiveness in order to make his highly original art a little more widely known. Several years ago E. E. Cummings wrote a brilliant war novel, *The Enormous Room*, certainly better, in my opinion and in a few others', than its predecessor of the sort by Dos Passos, or the excellent book by Thomas Boyd, which followed it. He is also a gifted painter after Pablo Picasso and a master of the line-drawing. To say the least, Mr. Cummings is the most versatile practitioner of three arts in this country.

Tulips and Chimneys, however, is not yet for the general reader any more than *Gaspard de la Nuit* of Aloysius Bertrand was accessible to the French public of his day. It seems that the lay reader of poetry must lag a generation or two behind any technical innovation in the art, until the more superficial violations of poetic convention get fairly well broadcast through the megaphone of popular education. To the complete novice, certainly, any stanza from even the comfortable Longfellow would seem monstrous at first glance (with each new line strangely initiating a capital letter whether or not a new thought-unit began there), until some influence of custom made such an artifice appear to be a matter of course. And here the preliminary difficulty in the poetry of Cummings arises. He doesn't begin his lines with capitals. In fact, he uses them at all only at unexpected places for emphasis and being nicely self-effacing he writes the first person personal pronoun with a small letter. Really, it all depends on what you're used to. Most people don't like to be shaken up and annoyed with what appear to be tricks, not of art but of print; but in these days when poetry, whatever its primitive origins in song, is so inescapably tied to the printed page, these novelties can't be a serious basis of rejection by serious critics. I proceed to his poetry.

The poetry of E. E. Cummings makes no pretentions to the kind of traditional profundity which the present generation has repudiated as sententious bathos. It invokes no metaphysical abstractions after the fashion of sanctioned English poetry and it employs the mythologies only when it is possible to make them the vehicle of the finest connotations; and to get at once to the point, the art of Mr. Cummings, within its limitations, is perfection. These limitations may be grave. First and last, Mr. Cummings is convicted of no positive illusion as to the ultimate meaning of the experience he has impeccably recorded in his poems; he has emotion, it is true, but he lacks passion. One may here recall the remark offered the great Baudelaire by Sainte-Beuve that that consummate verbal artificer rendered himself cold toward his very self by a too exacting analysis. And it isn't irrelevant to comment that Baudelaire, who with Poe asserted that the dimmest margins of thought could be expressed meaningfully by the great artist, is the father in technique of this new school of which E. E. Cummings is the cynosure.

For Mr. Cummings the inexpressible doesn't exist. I have said that he employs no metaphysical abstractions—words that have lost vitality by a long separation from physical objects. His poems are laboriously wrought, but simply presented, arrangements of naked observation into magnificent patterns, by the most lucid intelligence in modern poetry. His perception is as penetrating as the Roentgen ray and his vocabulary, which is so flexible that he is enabled actually to re-define, to contribute new meaning to every word he uses, is fully adequate to his minutest discoveries. His attitude, his dominant emotion is a preoccupation with sensuous Beauty and its destroyer, Time or Death. Take this, from "Songs":

> it is the autumn of a year:
> When through the thin air stooped with fear,

across the harvest whitely peer
empty of surprise
death's faultless eyes

He translates thought completely into intuition, into seeing; for his rhetoric isn't mere words like most of Swinburne's. Examine these phrases: "chattering sunset," "skating on noisy wheels of joy," "gasping organ waving moth-like tunes."

Mr. Cummings is master of a bewildering variety of forms: "Puella Mea," in tetrameters, is nearly too perfect; it takes one's breath. And the first poem in the volume, "Epithalamion," is in a new eight-line stanza as finely wrought as any in the whole range of English and American verse. The dauntless exuberance of imagery and subtlety of rhythm in the poem lead the reader irresistibly into Christopher Marlowe's "Hero and Leander." I hope my personal enthusiasm will justify quoting one stanza from the poem:

A silver sudden parody of snow
tickles the air to golden tears, and hark!
the flicker's laughing yet, while on the hills
the pines deepen to whispers primeval and throw
backward their foreheads to the barbarous bright
sky, and suddenly from the valley thrills
the unimaginable upward lark
and drowns the earth and passes into light

From the Nashville *Tennessean* (March 23, 1924)

DuBose Heyward

Skylines and Horizons, by DuBose Heyward. Macmillan, 1924.

SKYLINES AND HORIZONS does not introduce Mr. DuBose Heyward, for he has steadily claimed the attention of a considerable and for the most part appreciative audience for some years, through his contributions to the magazines, his activities in the Poetry Society of South Carolina, and, most notably, his collaboration with Mr. Allen in *Carolina Chansons.*

Mr. Heyward is a poet assured of a hearing both North and South. First he satisfied the expectancy of people out of the South as to what a Southern poet ought to be (he is intensely local, thoroughly of his immediate background and soil), and, second, he will stir to the point of enquiry those people of his own section, who have awaited, in these weary years, the appearance of a poet who should present an honest transcript of phases of the local scene, unsentimentalized, unwept, but not unsung.

They haven't awaited him in vain. Mr. Heyward is the looked-for interpreter. And if for no other claim than that of a generous and unprejudiced fidelity to his difficult, because hitherto mistreated, materials, Mr. Heyward may justly rank as the most important autochthonous poet in the South at the present time. I do not think, everything considered, that he is the foremost poet; but even though the professional reader, the technically minded critic, does discover certain deficiencies in Mr. Heyward as an artist, the discovery is hardly sufficient to support a denial of achievement to his work as a whole.

The first section of the volume, "Skylines," contains eleven poems which offer significant aspects of the life of the primitives in the

15

Great Smoky Mountains. "The Mountain Woman," "The Mountain
Preacher," "Black Christmas," "A Yoke of Steers," "A Mountain
Town," "The Mountain Graveyard," are titles that suggest the wide
range of Mr. Heyward's treatment. He finds the mountain people
locked in the prisonhouse of their own dumb suffering, from which
they have no escape of utterance or ampler living, where their characteristic attitude is a blindly protesting and inarticulate stoicism;
and these lines, perhaps better than any others, condense the spirit
of Mr. Heyward's mountain poems:

> In this deep moment, hushed and intimate,
> When the great hills lean close and understand,
> Where silence broods, and beauty is made plain,
> Children in life's dark house may swing a gate,
> That lets into a lucent, ample land
> Where lips struck dumb may learn to sing again.

These poems are convincing; the subordination of the poet's own
personality and his consequent immersion in the rich implications
of his scene enable him to select with fine deftness the significant
detail, the hidden but essential emotion, and this exacting imper-
sonality also enables him to make his selections, in most instances,
in terms of a rigorous objectivity. But not in all, for Mr. Heyward
has not been contented with a presentation of this "milieu" devoid
of all extraneous commentary; but in strict justice one must say
that the assumption of what amounts to a viewpoint in the presence
of materials like Mr. Heyward's was inevitable, and to say that Mr.
Heyward's commentary is often unpleasingly redundant is perhaps
only another way of saying that Mr. Heyward isn't Thomas Hardy.
    However, justice may lapse into mercy if exception isn't taken to
the last stanza of "The Mountain Graveyard," which is otherwise
the best poem of the mountain series. Here, there is a terrific simplicity of vision, the cemetery is at once the prospect and retrospect
of the people, and as the poem gathers in power the reader accumulates margins and suggestions and implications which at the end
of the last stanza but one, establish a unity of emotion almost overwhelming; but in the final stanza these suggestions and margins of
emotion, which it is the very essence of poetry to leave unex-

plained, are committed to definite terms which nullify entirely their capacity for excitement:

> Oh, they could call their dreams home from the sky.
> And carry beauty with them when they die.

All this was contained by implication in the poem and it shocks the reader to see it confined in terms which do not explain it but only fetter it. Again in strict justice, this is the most unsatisfactory case of Mr. Heyward's deficiency, and I indicate it out of no theoretical prepossession, only out of an actual sense of annoyance in reading the poem.

After all, and in spite of an authentic appeal of the mountain poems, we must turn to "Horizons," poems of the South Carolina low country, for the best of DuBose Heyward. Of these, "Chant for an Old Town" (already pleasantly familiar), "Horizons," "The Equinox," all are rich in local color and proclaim for their author an accurate imaginative appreciation of his landscape. "Buzzard Island," though perhaps attempting less than the others in the brief compass, seems to me to achieve more. It is a magnificent poem; it is the direct and powerful vision of the poet.

Skylines and Horizons is altogether a very important book. Its interpretation of the mountain people supersedes all the others in verse form; its presentation of the seacoast legends and landscapes is at once original and artistic. Though other poets in the South whose work is less obviously local may have a stronger claim to eminence than Mr. Heyward, he is, nevertheless, of the company of five or six whose gifts are of national rather than of purely sectional interest.

From the Nashville *Tennessean* (April 20, 1924)

Edwin Arlington Robinson

The Man Who Died Twice, by Edwin Arlington Robinson.
Macmillan, 1924.

THE APPEARANCE OF any book by Edwin Arlington Robinson is always an important event in contemporary American literature and, if one may believe a bit in signs, in the English scene as well. For precisely twenty-eight years Mr. Robinson has written in a vein of poetry so rich in the poetic mineral and so consistent in the quality of evenness of its yieldings that perhaps no other living American, if indeed there be any among the dead, can advance so strong a claim for first place among our poets.

Robinson is thoroughly aware of his duties as an artist, in his shorter poems at any rate; there, he is the master of the beautiful, if meagerly beautiful, line; and if he often evinces an idiosyncrasy somewhat questionably individual, he is seldom guilty of a whimsicality of which one of the uses is cleverness.

So much for the halting lucubrations of the reviewer; meaning little or nothing. For despite Mr. Robinson's unchallenged accession to authority, no one seems to know just why he deserves his undisputed laurel. In the presence of Mr. Robinson's poetry all critics appear to be helpless, singularly embarrassed. Mr. Middleton Murry of London, for example, announces his respect for Robinson, but isn't sure that he is a poet: he may be some sort of psychologist or other; however, he is very important.

I submit that the English critic's dictum amounts only to a confession of perplexity: it gets us no nearer a critical handle to take hold of Mr. Robinson. Nevertheless, it may supply us with a key to help unlock the secret of his power and, likewise, his occasional lack of it. Mr. Robinson is said to be a psychologist.

And this accounts, I suppose, for the grim exactions his poetry makes of the reader's attention; he is a different poet, to be followed narrowly. The reader is quite equal to the task in the shorter character poems; the span of attention isn't greatly strained; the poet can sustain his intensity in a very dramatic fashion through a poem of only relative length. For example, the familiar "Flammonde," or the poem which I think is his best, "The Mill." But what about the longer poems? The Arthurian poems, "The Man Against the Sky," even "Captain Craig"? What is the reason of their tedium, as distinguished from the nearly breathless excitement of the shorter poems? For Mr. Robinson has written always in the same idiom, with the same peculiar oxymoron of statement; both divisions of his work are unmistakably from the same hand; so why is this difference felt?

It is simply, I believe, that Mr. Robinson's genius, like Landor's, is not meant to be exercised in the long poem. But the English poet John Donne was quite as difficult as Robinson, it may be objected, yet he wrote long poems which never flagged. But there is a difference; Donne is everywhere present, almost excruciatingly, in his work; Robinson never reveals himself, never gives himself away. What does Mr. Robinson think of his characters? He doesn't say, overtly. Instead, in his long poems he merely presents series after series of abstruse and perhaps exact analyses of successive mental states. His people never act, never do anything; they only think, feel, suffer; and the things in the outer world that make them suffer are utterly left out in his report of them; they are just so many abstracted minds. But how about Henry James? Was he not equally subjective, did he not create mere animated ideas? Yes; but James was a novelist, he was circumstantial, he gave his characters place and time; there was movement, drama. In Mr. Robinson there is no drama; there is no action that draws his men and women into a unity. Whether this be a damaging limitation of the more pretentious side of Mr. Robinson's art, the long poem, I am not prepared to say; but I think it is undeniably a characteristic of it.

The Man Who Died Twice is one of Robinson's long character-poems. And there is much fine poetry in it, many beautiful lines:

> They had come,
> And in their coming had remembered only
> That they were messengers, who like himself
> Had now no choice; and they were telling him this
> In the last language of mortality,
> Which has no native barrier but the grave.

But too much of the tortured probing, as follows, is the very thing that renders suspect, at times, even Mr. Robinson's psychology:

> . . . he would have been as one
> Who cared no more, having had everything,
> Where there was no more caring.

Of this there is but an occasional leavening in seventy-nine pages.

But an "unfavorable review" of any volume from Edwin Arlington Robinson would be highly disrespectful: it is the reviewer's business, I take it, to make only a provisional distinction, a tentative classification of a new work. Finality is the office of criticism proper, as is also the discussion of a poet's spiritual and philosophical tendencies—a discussion that can be carried on only through reference to the poet's work as a whole.

From the Nashville *Tennessean* (May 4, 1924)

Negro Poetry

An Anthology of Negro Poetry, edited with a Critical Introduction, Biographical Sketches of the Authors, and Biographical Notes by Newman Ivey White and Walter Clinton Jackson. Trinity College Press, 1924.

PROFESSORS WHITE AND JACKSON have compiled a very useful anthology of American Negro verse, which covers the entire period of Negro literary activity from its beginning in Phyllis Wheatley down to Countee P. Cullen, a young man of 20 years, now a student in New York University.

The bulk of American Negro poetry is not accessible to the general reader; and although in the past two or three years the present volume has had its predecessors, notably *The Book of American Negro Poetry* by James Weldon Johnson, himself a gifted Negro, it represents, nevertheless, the first significant attempt on the part of white critics to do justice to Negro literature in America. It is perhaps just as well that the entirety of poetry in this field of American literature isn't generally available, for, as the editors of this book say, it is on the whole pretty worthless, and the good would probably be submerged in the fatigue resulting from the labor of reading so much that is bad; so the most obvious merit of this new anthology is that it represents only 34 authors out of a period of a hundred and fifty years and thus enables the layman, or the critic whose interest is elsewhere, to see for himself a certain degree of achievement in the Negro race in the literature of poetry.

It is impossible for this reviewer to form any definite estimate as to whether the editors might have made a better selection of poems, but it is only just to infer that they would not have been interested in Negro writing cast in the less conventional forms. In the introduction, under the heading, "General Conclusions," Professor White says by way of indicating a fair prospect for the future of Negro poetry: "Braithwaite has already passed beyond it (i.e., the racial inferiority complex) and a wider cultural horizon for other Negroes will have the same results that it had for American Literature." In short, the complete assimilation of American culture will equip the Negro with the "refinement" and "taste" requisite to writing in a tradition utterly alien to his temperament, but this is pointed to optimistically as a thing greatly to be desired. Of Joseph Seaman Cotter, Jr., Professor White says: "Fire, perhaps he lacked, but . . . innate good taste and intellectual background he possessed to a degree unusual among the poets his race has so far produced."

This of Claude McKay: "Some of his poems are too erotic for good taste and conventional morality." Whose good taste and whose morality? If the business of criticism is partly concerned with giving the creative impulse intelligent direction, I would warn Negro artists in this country not to take too seriously Professor White's conception of culture. By subscribing to it the Negro might become a "nice" person and an upholder of backwoods morality, but he would lose his genius.

It is therefore not difficult to see why the editors of this book place Dunbar and Braithwaite (who is only Negro by an accident of blood and has as little of the Negro temperament as Longfellow) above Claude McKay. Repeated reference is made to the "finish" of those writers. And it is still easier to understand why they overlooked altogether the work of Jean Toomer. Toomer is the finest Negro literary artist that has yet appeared in the American scene, but he is interested in the interior of Negro life, not in the pressure of American culture on the Negro.

From the Nashville *Tennessean* (August 3, 1924)

John Crowe Ransom

Chills and Fever, by John Crowe Ransom. Alfred A. Knopf, 1924.

IT WAS REMARKED of old and has been repeated anew that the business of poets is indicated in the gerund Seeing. But particular ages subjugate abstract saws to particular needs. The 19th Century, strangely prefering Latinity, got Vision out of Seeing and produced, for example, Tennyson. Tennyson until recently has been misjudged; he saw marvellous things; a morality that impoverished the spirit, but he of course made up for it by seeing "the heavens full with commerce, argosies of magic sails", that were spread in the interest of a materialistic Romanticism then long under way and lately brought to its lugubrious profits in the War. There is another way of seeing—things as they are, the Classical way. Mr. Ransom's poems are essentially in the Classical tradition, compromised here and there by certain impurities.

Some obvious characters to be thought of in the presence of Classical art are precision, objectivity, humility, restraint; in other words, the repudiation of a rhetorical Infinite in which the megalomania of man rhetorically participates. Mr. Ransom's *Weltanschauung* may be described this way. And a typical quotation from the present volume reveals an essence nearer to that of H. D. or Carmen CI of Catullus than to the poems of the cerebral Romantic John Donne whom he doubtless resembles superficially—that is, in diction, in unexpected contexts for old words.

> I have a grief
> (It was not stolen like a thief),
> Albeit I have no bittern by the lake
> To cry it up and down the brake.

23

....
I will be brief,
Assuredly I have a grief
And I am shaken; but not as a leaf.

When Mr. Ransom's first book came out in 1919, *Poems About God*, somebody reviewing it spoke of a growing "cult of brutality" (the cult hasn't been heard of since). The point exploited the cleverness of American criticism: cleverness gets at differences but not distinctions. Mr. Ransom's work was different, in a certain department—cult, if you will have it so—of Modernism, because it didn't have aesthetic hysteria over every roadside buttercup. Its efficiencies lay in what the pedantry of reviewers names slovenly technique; but in what sense was it slovenly? Mr. Ransom's present "technique" is imperfect, occasionally jagged; there are loose ends and often a deplorable inaccuracy and mixture of diction (see lines 7 and 8 of "Fall of Leaf"). Now, as in 1919, John Crowe Ransom is a poet orientating his perception of the field of the Immediate—not the *petite sensation*, but under the conviction that the proper study of man is man, classically proper; but he is encumbered with the properties of an outworn and, for his purposes, irrelevant Romantic tradition. The thoroughgoing Classicist in contemporary American verse is William Carlos Williams: precision, objectivity, restraint, etc. And it is safe to say that Mr. Ransom, in fundamental intention, is closer to Williams than he is to most of the poets who write, as Ransom does, in "rhyme and metre." But Classicism in Anglo-American criticism means the part of Alexander Pope which is the trees, forgetting the true woods of Classicism altogether. Mr. Ransom's impurities are not to be impeached through an approach to his technical equipment; it must be said that he fails of his complete intention in missing the precision that would make his Classical spirit aesthetically significant. Take this:

> "Dick, they found the ending good,
> The Babes who ventured in the wood.
> So tell the leaves that die and fall,
> As we lie a-shiver,
> Stop and stitch us one close pall
> To hide us deep forever."

This is entirely Romantic vocabulary and is a rather trivial symbolism, excessive and blurred, for a spirit that elsewhere has only a few leanings with a Romantic Baudelaire toward Mystery—*l'expansion des choses infinies.* The same subject-matter gets better treatment in another poem, "Spectral Lovers." Mr. Ransom is in a pleasant middle marsh on his way from the thicket to clean meadow.

Yet there is no other verse in America just like John Crowe Ransom's. If one put aside the attempt to relate his work categorically to one of the two main streams of literature—an attempt slightly out-of-date but perhaps still serviceable—it is easily distinguished for subtlety of wit, ranging from a seemingly naive irony to impatient satire, and for a personal idiom flexible enough to carry these qualities to a variety of effects, often brilliant and always individual. There is a deftly casual neatness and surprise of rhythm in poems like "Here Lies a Lady" and "Bells for John Whiteside's Daughter." "Armageddon" and "Judith of Bethulia" are rich patterns of poetic texture, largely effective through a new management of echo and half rhyme. The only obvious mistakes in the book are a few poems that tend to a harsh, indecisive lyricism: an impurity I have already tried to define.

Altogether, *Chills and Fever* evinces a mind detached from the American scene and mostly nurtured from England, indifferent to the current mania of critics for writers who "express America." If it articulates no deep essentiality of experience, it is a lucid commentary, whose properties aren't very detectable critically, on the shifting surfaces of experience. And it points, throughout, to a performance, more fundamental in vision and purer in method, yet to come.

From *The Guardian* (November, 1924)

A Literary Letter from New York

LITERARY COMMUNICATIONS from New York in November can hardly deserve the name of literary intelligence. The fall book lists, it is true, display a great deal to the interest of the most catholic readers—poetry, fiction, biography, criticism; but one must avoid a too facile characterization of the whole season on the partial evidence of its beginnings. One recalls, in the realm of verse alone three surprises that came late last year, books by the different and excellent poets Cummings and Davidson and Auslander. And caution is further justified in the promise of a new book by Mr. Cummings which is already being set up by the only printer in America, it is said, who can render an accurate typography for the verbal zigzags and gyroscopes of his sometimes bad, often beautiful, always amazing verse. Fiction and biography will doubtless offer surprises of their own.

But at the moment the present writer happens to be preoccupied with poetry. It is a great pleasure to transmit a composite enthusiasm, stronger, of course, in the more conservative cliques (everything is cliques and politics in literary New York), which pays high tribute to the recent book by Mr. John Crowe Ransom. When one surveys the contemporary scene, one is easily convinced that *Chills and Fever* is the most distinguished book of verse yet published this fall by an American. There are, to be sure, *Heliodora* by H.D. and the brilliant new-Elizabethanism by the Australian*, Roy Campbell, in *The Flaming Terrapin*; but these books are not by Americans, H.D. now being thoroughly settled in England. Thus one need only select at random a current book by an "established poet," as

*South African

Miss Harriet Monroe would say in Social-Register fashion, to visualize the defection of the elderly in the present season and the accession of the young; I refer to the typically inferior book by Edgar Lee Masters.

Poetical activity in the wider sense, which includes the interesting work of the magazines, appears to be on a high plane. It is vigorous, almost indomitable. But it is chaotic in its public approach, scattered, and thus to a large extent futile; for who reads the poetry journals? Surely not many of the poets themselves.

Too many magazines, too many groups—it is almost Parisian in this respect—all of them, or nearly all, possessing, however, a few stars to boast of, they are without exception encumbered with the obligation to present not only the stars but their "friends," good and bad, and the stars are usually obscured by misty nonentities. There seems to be a murmur of dissatisfaction everywhere—except among those who write agreeably of literature and care little about it.

The growing snobbism of the once-esteemed *Dial*, its obvious dilettantism in printing the exotic confections of Miss Elizabeth Coatsworth not once, through error, but repeatedly, or the marrowless echoes of James Stephens' European reputation, leaves the field open to a journal that would substitute letters for a hobby.

A new magazine is needed, one that would serve American letters as *The Criterion* serves English by being actually international instead of nostalgic for alien cultures for their own sake. It is a commonplace of long standing that no poet offers his work to the *Century* or *Scribner's* or *The Bookman*, or almost any other journal but the *Yale Review*, unless he must sell his tamest poem in order to buy a meal or pay room rent in a crumbling tenement somewhere off Bleecker Street. But the virtue patience, in going through the jungle of magazines, brings more than its own reward; it occasionally discloses poetry of a high order. Thus, the most interesting poets this season in books or out, regardless of style, school, or locality, are Mr. Cummings and Mr. Ransom, Mr. Hart Crane and Mr. Yvor Winters—and Miss Marianne Moore. You will not find their poems in *The Bookman* or *Harper's*; nor, for that matter, in Miss Monroe's *Poetry*. You will read them in the *Transatlantic Review*, *The Fugitive*, *The Measure*, *1924*. The young writers who contrived to print in *Broom* and *Secession*, both defunct, some indifferent writing and more of much distinction have apparently moved in a body to *1924*, published by Edwin Seaver in Woodstock. This little journal has printed writing that has got for it the approval of Herbert Read in England, who says it is the most important organ critically in America, and it has also received the anathema of pure billingsgate from Mr. Ernest Boyd in this country. To those who know the seamy aspects of Mr. Boyd his attack on these young writers might conceivably advertise considerable merit for them prior to any reading of their work; Mr. Boyd is wholly vulgar, partly dishonest; his attack, placed as it is on the journalistic plane of personality rather than on the critical plane of literature, runs through all the devices of his trade, touching acutely every stop of popular suspicion of literature. Boyd's attack is doubly effective. On the one hand, since these young writers aren't quickly understood by people, he gives the well-meaning bank clerks who read *The Bookman* and the miseducated sophisticates who make a canticle of the *American Mercury*, a chance to feel vaguely, but hugely superior to that one thing it is most convenient to feel superior to—what one doesn't understand. On the other hand, he gains the applause of the interested parties now in literary power, a professor like Phelps and his editorial soul-mate, John Farrar, because he sets up another and needed prop in the creaking bulwark of somewhat ignorant and wholly jealous authority. Mr. Boyd is obviously the Celtic literary man who has become an efficient American journalist.

In spite of this and that and what not, Mr. Waldo Frank is still writing. And still more important at the moment, Mr. Kenneth Burke has written, in *The White Oxen*, the most noteworthy, the soundest prose book to appear so far this season. But I shall wait and do it a better measure of justice in a full-length review. And Mr. Glenway Wescott's *The Apple of the Eye* must rank as the purely stylistic achievement of the year; one is almost certain nothing will surpass it in the spring.

From the Nashville *Tennessean* (December 7, 1924)

Edgar Lee Masters

The New Spoon River, by Edgar Lee Masters. Boni and Liveright, 1924.

A "GENERATION" in letters usually consists in a number of writers whose aims are largely the same. About 1912 or before, there came into prominence in America certain novelists and poets, and two critics of power—Brooks and Mencken—whose vision of this country was directed by the same general sense of social and moral values, by a similar critical intolerance of the so-called puritan tradition, of its incomplete evaluation of the spiritual life and its consequent neglect of the aesthetic motive in literature. So vehement were these writers in the act of liberation—perhaps stung to revolt by a memory of the pioneer, Stephen Crane—that little time or insight was given to the avowed purpose of their attack: aesthetic freedom from academic moralism. Whether any of these men could have achieved a mature art-form out of the immense documentary evidence which Dreiser, for instance, produced is an impossible question; it is simply a fact that none of them did. And because Edgar Lee Masters was the significant poet of the movement, the measure of its success as a spiritual, aesthetically realized tableau of an epoch in America may be found in his books. Mr. Masters, like most of his contemporaries, never mastered the art of writing; and his books, so soon as 1925, claim the critical interest—critical habit aside—only as history, as evidence on one side in the ethical history of the United States. For our moral values, if not radically different, are at least greatly changed in fifteen years. And with this alteration, this more precise realization of a moral direction, Mr. Masters becomes solely of documentary importance. He has never been an artist.

Now Mr. Masters returns, after some years of not very excellent novel-writing, to the subject-matter he was beginning to exploit about fifteen years ago: he returns to Spoon River. At first Mr. Masters was interesting. There was no criterion in America at that time to point out that his writing was sensational, very much as scandal among neighbors is important in communities where such matters are not accepted but are precariously discussed; he shouted the bloody truth. It was hardly an aesthetic interest that held one when one read about a spinster who confessed she hadn't been a virgin since puberty . . . Confessions, perhaps, aren't so interesting as they were; nor is the revelation of vice, or of sentimentalized struggle for emancipation, very morally significant to the incurious. Yet Mr. Masters was acclaimed a worthy poet . . . even a great one, mainly by those who introduced him—Reedy and Miss Monroe and Mr. Mencken. Now Mr. Mencken suspects Mr. Masters of occasional dulness. *The New Spoon River* is oppressively dull.

Edgar Lee Masters was astute enough to appropriate for a new matter a well-known old form. But whether because he wasn't sufficiently sensitive to find out all its possibilities or because he didn't care about poetry he failed to make it, and thus his subject-matter, of lasting importance. Nobody had used the form in America before; almost nobody had read the *Characters* of Theophrastus, and the vague journalism which advertised Mr. Masters' annual reading of the Greek Anthology now seems rather meaningless, for the journalists hadn't examined the models—it was easier to talk about them for Mr. Masters' benefit. So he went on to greatness, not through poetry but through Freud when Freudians were comparatively rare.

There are certain obvious properties of the epitaphic monologue that may be used mechanically for correspondingly obvious effects. Mr. Masters' effects reduce to one: the irony in the discrepancy between surface appearance and inner actuality. The irony is established dramatically through the delivery of the actuality from the grave and the simultaneous destruction by it of the appearance which was the life of the character. This is a formula for tragedy.

But Masters, never exceeding the formula, produced in his epitaphs merely a series of moral situations, pure when he effaced himself, false when he made the character a mouthpiece for his own expanding messiah-complex. In neither of the Spoon River books are there more than two or three "poems" in which the imagination is carried to a realm of overtones, to the essences rationally indeterminate, which are poetry: to the interplay of free sensations in excess of the terms of the moral situation which is the scaffolding of the poem. Yet this aesthetic deficiency was largely compensated for by ingenuity. Mr. Masters constructed a whole town, with its complete moral interrelations; and in the interrelation of many persons a single person lived and apparently became at the end more than a tragic homily on the frustrations of his own life. Few of the poems were complete of themselves; almost every one depended for its effectiveness on the memory of others; the weaknesses, the bad writing, in an individual poem were covered up by the complex interdependency of characters in the whole. This interdependency created various tangents for speculation beyond the limits of the moral problem furnished by the separate poem; but the tangents were extensions of the moral problem only (never giving a free direction to the imagination) though they seemed to be poetry; upon analysis they disperse and break down. Through the persistent use of this device Mr. Masters has given us for some years a spurious product which satisfies his own generation—as poetry should satisfy men in all times.

And the properties of the *New Spoon River* are the properties of the old. But Mr. Masters has in this book, as in his first one, fallen into an occasional lyricism, rough but very pure. There are two, only two, notable specimens in this volume, "Howard Lemsom" and "Gordon Halicha." They are notable no less as two exceptions in an astonishing mass of tedium.

Whatever the dissatisfaction one may have felt after reading through the old Spoon River, one is certain to prefer it to the new. The writer more frequently had his eye upon his matter, was more nearly the poet. But now Mr. Masters, along with others of his generation, has become the very person they all thought they detested—the moralist. It was a question of Whose Morals. And now that Mr. Masters' moral preferences are more or less exposed, it is impossible for one to be concerned with his issues. A vague though extremely active contempt for certain permanent vices in human nature—hypocrisy, meanness, malice—is not the entire prerequisite toward informing a system of definite moral values. So his protest is scattered into a morally revolting haze of ontology, objurgation, prophecy, that he probably kept bottled up until he became so convinced of his vision that he had to give it with some ill-humor and much arrogance to the world. Lacking the intelligence to diagnose precisely the social evils, the cultural astigmatism of the people of his Spoon River, he has come to hate them in the consciousness of an obscurely superior self. Those who would be messiahs should remember, perhaps, that contempt for men and a vulgar admiration for the appurtenances of culture had no place in the ethics of Buddha or Christ or Lao-tse. And if we shall have messiahs . . . when the half-gods go, the gods—sometimes—arrive.

From *The Guardian* (May–June, 1925)

The Sitwells

The Thirteenth Caesar, by Sacheverell Sitwell. George H. Doran Company, 1925.
Out of the Flame, by Osbert Sitwell. George H. Doran Company, 1925.

FOR NEARLY a decade the three Sitwells have been the most effectual antagonists of the poets who rather too often dilute the English tradition into Georgian anthologies and prove to their own ease that a safe repetition of threadbare properties, with the approval of Mr. Gosse, is better than the timidest formation of the literary conscience into a living poetry. The Wheels poets have recorded their opposition in considerable direct invective, interesting, perhaps, quite out of proportion to the intrinsic value attaching to the mediocrities they have satirized. But they have justified this assumption of the rôle of Archilochus among the blockheads of an age by producing a limited quantity of distinguished verse, most of it in the books of Miss Edith Sitwell.

These poets and Mr. Aldous Huxley, in his *Leda*, had at least one more preoccupation in common than their interest in Rimbaud and Laforgue, and T. S. Eliot's assertion that "novelty is preferable to repetition": they had the immediately available example of the poems of Mr. Eliot himself. And although they have with the integrity of good writers avoided imitating one another, they have Mr. Eliot to acknowledge for much of their discipline and themselves to censure for an excessive pictorial imagery which continually betrays them into a monotonously attenuated rewriting of their own poems. But exception, by way of indicating a distinction for further use, must be entered for Miss Sitwell, who more than any other young English poet integrates the extensions of her intuition in a fully realized visual world, small but entirely her own: yet even in Miss Sitwell, at her worst, pure fantasy roots the correspondences out of any definitely perceivable world, and since her mind doesn't move toward large conceptual structures, her poetry is occasionally only a metallic rigidity of phrase, pleasing at first, then scattering and unsatisfactory.

This distinction, in different terms, must be even more carefully applied to the work of Mr. Sacheverell Sitwell. He speaks of his world as the "glass world of metaphor"—a world rich from an observation of the slighter aspects of nature, a static world without life or process of its own where Mr. Sitwell's eye stops for a transition which suggests the terms of a symbol for a sudden shift of feeling. This world is not, however, like his sister's or Wallace Stevens's, intellectualized—"I know a tree that bears a semblance to the thing I have in mind," says Mr. Stevens. Mr. Sacheverell Sitwell's "New Water Music," for example, progresses through no other unity of vision than that implied by the title of the poem; it is pure reverie in the lack of emotional impulsion or of a severely intellectual design. Indeed, most of his poetry lacks form; for his interest in *feelings* almost to the exclusion of *emotions* forces him to neglect economy and forego direction. There is no evidence of conscious use of an intellectual formula, which may be called Mallarmé's: a selection of metaphors perceptually mixed but leading to a conceptual end realized in the structure of the poem as a whole. Yet the best work in *The Thirteenth Caesar* has precisely this effect because the best poems, with an exception in "Doctor Donne and Gargantua," are short and thus, since Mr. Sitwell has taste, there is no excess of material to destroy the effect, if not a deliberate intention, of control:

> Two apples tumbled from a bough
> Your breasts show, lying clear,
> And straight the swans begin to plough
> Till furrows do appear:
> Now with their beaks the fruit they try
> And air, like glass, breaks with a cry.

This, from "The Venus of Bolsover Castle," and the four "Variations" possess this quality. But apparently only a definitely limited theme, with limited sources of imagery, rescues such work from sheer decoration.

Mr. Osbert Sitwell's poetry has less decorative value than his brother's, and proceeds from an emotional centre outward: it represents a closer coördination of a few permanent emotional attitudes with an appropriate symbolism. It is at once more solid and less brilliant.

But the Sitwell brothers have enough in common to share the same limitations: a pictorial imagery which, in Sacheverell, diffuses in a brilliant indecisive reverie and, in Osbert, projects the emotion into an arresting exoticism and richness which in its own simplicity it doesn't have. The result in both, with differences, is absence of emotional conviction, and decoration.

The properties of decoration were exploited by the French seventeenth century and the English eighteenth. There is much of it in Pope. But there is very little of it in the Romantic poetry of any age; for it thrives only in a society emotionally unambitious, in which an imaginative conquest of a universe is less important than immediate social relations and allegiances. The decay of the Romantic movement has delivered poets into a world rather tired emotionally, suspicious of the Romantic preoccupation with a doubtful Infinite. And they are deprived of capacity for the kind of allegiance that enabled Pope, who knew a rascal when he saw one, to write sympathetically of Villiers because Villiers stood for the foundation of his society—Church and State. Were there available in England a similar social temper in which Mr. Sacheverell Sitwell might participate, one could imagine him writing

> The George and Garter dangling from that bed
> Where tawdry yellow strove with dirty red,
> Great Villiers lies . . .

As it is, Mr. Osbert Sitwell's satires—effective satire equally with encomium implying, by negation, a fixed order for attention—are scattered against a number of dull "society ladies" and persons who might enjoy Georgian poetry and admire Kipling. The Sitwell brothers, interesting enough as expert craftsmen in minor modes, are producing mostly decoration and lack direction entirely. They are neo-classical sensibilities without a milieu.

From *The New Republic* (July 29, 1925)

Charles Williams, Æ, Archibald MacLeish

Windows of Night, by Charles Williams. Oxford University Press, 1925.
Voices of the Stones, by Æ. The Macmillan Company, 1925.
The Pot of Earth, by Archibald MacLeish. Houghton Mifflin Company, 1925.

CONTEMPORARY ENGLISH poetry seems to be a much clearer field for an easy criticism of classification and partial definition than any other living body of verse with which an American critic is likely to be concerned. At this time France offers a difficulty of another order—that of many active second rate minds and nearly as many schools of hazardous existence, whose rivalries are so eccentric from the main issues of poetry that the schools detain one, less as solutions of their problems than as symptoms of an important change actually conducted by a poet like Paul Valéry: yet to have exhibited M. Valéry has been an achievement carrying all the seriousness of mature art. M. Valéry and Mr. W. B. Yeats are precisely the persons England of this generation has not produced. For without a single major talent to assimilate those elements of the historical literary experience suited to a new scientific construction of the universe, or to the social implications of that construction, English poetry may be said merely to discourse in three principal tendencies, each with a history: the Wheels group, at its best in Eliot, whom it doesn't formally include; the Georgians, from whom Wheels revolted about ten years ago; and the Conservationists, whose cosmic and rhetorical machinery was scrapped by the revolutionist Mr. Masefield, a founder of Georgianism, in 1911, when he "threatened"—according to Stephen Phillips—"the standards of English Poetry." The history is indispensable: Mr. Charles Williams can be understood only as an anachronism; but he deserves, for that extrinsic reason, to be understood.

For Mr. Williams's verse belongs to this last and conservative tendency. The school now lacks the authority of a great figure—a fact illuminating enough—but it still carries a wide public prestige through Phillips's standards of English Poetry which are the current popular taste; that is to say, through the Divine Right of Poesy. Mr. Williams conceives the poet as Vates, as seer of good and evil, of their joint or divergent progress in successive generations of the heart of Man. He scolds modern Doubt in many lines, some of them graceful in a synthetic melody put together from the rhetorical Victorian poets, nearly all of them devoid of artistic value—empty of the vitality attached to words only by a very alert experience of either books or living. For Mr. Williams, experience, which ordinarily participates in every creative intuition of a good poet, were better silent before the superior incentive of Inspiration. It is

> wise Mnemosyne
> Gravely to poets their vocation metes.

The use of Mnemosyne makes a capital point. As the type of degenerate artist Mr. Williams, having inherited a symbol, ignores its status as such and turns it into an efficient entity; so that the symbol of memory, like the "efficient God" in the Occasionalism of Malebranche, is supposed to work for the poet in defection of the psychological operations of memory. Mr. Williams would fail to see that James Joyce and Proust, without invoking Mnemosyne, are the only writers of this century who have creatively defined her. His production is fundamentally a piece of ironical levity unconsciously performed, set against the English tradition in all its distinguished phases: solemn, it lacks seriousness altogether. Dulness comes close to vulgarity.

Æ's poetry lacks seriousness but it is always supported by conviction. It does not crucify taste: it projects what is after all a world, the peculiar function of Æ's sensibility, and there is no false intuition of another or merely rhetorical world to corrupt the pattern. His world is the stasis of mysticism. The mystical vision, proceeding usually in one of two ways, attempts either to unfold a permanent order momently out of the currency of particular experiences, defining sameness in a rich variety, like Blake's, or to locate and define that order prior to and outside consciousness, like Plato's. The difference is ultimately the one between a creative and a philosophical satisfaction. The latter is Æ's and it means that as a poet he is vastly separate from his world, with only a few symbols fixedly and repetitiously available for connection with it. The power of his emotion everywhere overflows the meagre symbolic equipment; it isn't concentrated, like Blake's, wholly in the symbols at his disposal; his poetry is thus in the end a cold experience. The emotion scatters and only a contemplation remains. The tremendous conviction that has marked Æ's poetry from its beginning has not had the justice done it of a perfectly realized art. He is very serious about his conviction; he is indifferent to the seriousness of poetry.

But Mr. Archibald MacLeish's *The Pot of Earth* is one of the best books of verse printed in the last season, one of the three or four indications that capable new artists are at work in this country. It is derivative of blank-verse passages in *The Waste Land*: the excess of suspended rhythmical periods in long sequences of run-on lines, depriving the verse of solidity, makes one suspect that Mr. MacLeish rather unwisely studied Mr. Eliot's very personal use of Webster's and Ford's textures without having given much attention to the models themselves. But he has a thorough understanding of his material, the growth of a girl into a woman cast in terms of the parallel process in the vegetation rites described by James Frazer. This framework is nicely elaborated in an adequately controlled structure, an arrangement of detail in a beautifully suggestive subordination and emphasis. One is occasionally disturbed by an attenuation of metaphor that escapes the pattern and disrupts the unity of attention; but this fault usually attends the formation of an idiom. Mr. MacLeish is evidently in process of inventing a distinguished poetic language. He has written an interesting poem; it is probable that he will write an important one.

From *The New Republic* (October 14, 1925)

Conrad Aiken

Priapus and the Pool, by Conrad Aiken. Boni and Liveright, 1925.
Senlin: A Biography, by Conrad Aiken. London: The Hogarth Press, 1925.

MOST OF Conrad Aiken's poetry has possessed an excellence unimpeachably its own. This excellence has been accompanied by others out of the poetry of several contemporaries—two poems by Mr. Eliot alone, "Prufrock" and "La Figlia Che Piange," have informed much of his work with an attitude—and one suspects that, after all, he may have received too much attention. Yet he has deserved some; for he is almost the only living American poet who has satisfactorily developed a personal experience within the obvious metrical possibilities of certain lyrical forms. It is probable that Mr. Aiken has written as many as a dozen distinguished lyrics—a surprising achievement for any one in that genre—but the key to his failures in the more ambitious schemes, like *Senlin*, seems to lie in an explanation of his repetitiousness, of his diffuseness.

Mr. Aiken cannot with any conviction sustain an idea through its elaborations in a long poem. *Priapus and the Pool* and *Senlin* are collections of detached lyrics: the sole unifying character in such poems is the external pattern of a theme which remains, throughout, a point of reference and does not become an interior motivation giving the work form. Too often Mr. Aiken discards his sensibility to meet the demands of this pattern; and this means, of course, that since he rejects the rhythms of his own sensation his poetry seldom has internal rhythm and proceeds solely as a metrical contrivance. Thus there is a great deal of rhetorical padding in his work—which is to say, there is diffuseness. When Mr. Aiken cannot place his emotion in definite perceptions he scatters it with a decorative phrase:

40

> Into the azure world I call my heart . . .

Complex states of consciousness and conflicts of powerful feeling he usually avoids by appealing to their supposedly cosmic implications:

> Senlin, walking before us in the sunlight,
> Bending his long legs in a peculiar way,
> Goes to his work with thoughts of the universe.

"Universe" occurs too frequently in his poetry, and too significantly. But Mr. Aiken is indubitably the poet in his gift of pictorial visualization:

> . . . the blue hills
> Flashing like dolphins under a light like rain.

Only, he does not assimilate his vision with an emotion, with a subject-matter.

For Mr. Aiken, along with other gifted modern poets, has not found an important subject matter at all. Mr. Eliot has a *pointilliste* brilliance and at the same time his work is obscure in its totality; perceptually very sensitive, he cannot relate his sensation to a material more intimate than a philosophy of the present state of European culture, a subject matter that doubtless can never be comfortably elucidated by any American. Though now living in England Mr. Aiken is not appreciably aware of this problem in his poetry, but if he were, through even some very personal extension of it, his work might be at once less thinly diffuse and laudably more obscure. This is not said in the wish that he should become another sort of poet; simply that he needs, and deserves, to be a better one.

From The Nation (January 13, 1926)

Léonie Adams

Those Not Elect, by Léonie Adams. Robert M. McBride and Company, 1925.

MISS ADAMS'S first volume of poems contains such richness in familiar varieties that one might succeed in defining her quality analytically, in many instances phrase by phrase, with quotations from songs out of plays by Ford or Webster, and from Herbert and Carew. One should not expect to find Miss Adams after 1650— nor before the lyrics in *The Broken Heart*. Her poetry lacks the eighteenth-century interest in the object noted but not seen—

> A pair of garters, half a pair of gloves,
> And all the trophies of his former loves

—and it lacks the line by line simplicity of the early Elizabethan song:

> Pack clouds away and welcome day,
> With night we banish sorrow.

Her sensibility, metaphysical in Johnson's sense, has isolated a world somewhere between eighteenth-century decoration and the fresh intensity of a lyric by Thomas Heywood or Greene. For all her aptness in certain early sixteenth-century conventions—typically the subjective dialogue, in her "Death and the Lady"—the fusion of her qualities brings her closer to Carew than to any other poet. This, again, in spite of a Shakespearean idiom in some of her sonnets:

> Since now most precious mines can give no gold
> So absolute but it's made metaphor.

42

But Miss Adams, without any of the older classical machinery, more intensely visualizes and relates her images; she expresses herself in her best poems in terms of something impersonal and beyond conviction—an intense awareness of *things*. Her probing intensity is a little like that of her contemporary, Louise Bogan. Thus she does not exploit the extended intellectuality of Donne; her intelligence acts within its immediate problems. Her poetry is not an exhibit; it is quiet, serious, static. This last quality is a fixed relation between her and her world; she is not philosophically ambitious. "Never, being damned, see Paradise," writes Miss Adams in the title poem; it is the subject matter of all the verse in this book. Wit, or its current version in dandyism, is a quality that Miss Adams has rejected for a more serious irony; having accepted her own intricately derived world, she doesn't attempt to refute its terms. She is serious without an inversion of sentimentality.

Her irony designs the contexture of her perceptions; it is not a property.

> Now is my very marrow gone to dreaming,
> And I am stricken by its dream's precision
> To live bewildered between blood and seeming.

Her poetry becomes purer, if less directly exciting, when this irony, nearly always introspective, vanishes in a strict contemplation of its "objective reference"—in an absorption in the object itself.

> And if a lark shook out his wing,
> That shadow on your cheek I found.
> . . . .
> Now on dark wounds falls dreamily,
> Like a celestial dew, the snow.

Some of the personal, aesthetically unresolved confusion of these two ways of seeing persists, and Miss Adams has written fewer successful poems than an adept artificer of magazine verse would let himself write. Miss Adams is personal, meticulous, detached from ulterior literary motives; a distinguished limited sensibility, she is a distinguished minor poet. There are perhaps five poems in this book of almost ultimate perfection. But the many unrealized poems are honorably committed. She is conscious of a problem in poetic values, and her failures in integrity are worth considerably more than the neat reconstructions of properties into which several of her women contemporaries, after their first interesting successes, have been quickly diverted.

From *The Nation* (March 3, 1926)

Genevieve Taggard

Words for the Chisel, by Genevieve Taggard. Alfred A. Knopf, 1926.

MISS TAGGARD is one of four or five women poets who in the last five years have won a dignified popularity, and she is particularly distinguished in having written consistently better than any of them. She is the best craftsman. Her work is intelligently sustained; it is economical; her material emerges in clean, essential outlines. The artistic aim indicated by the title of the present volume would be pretentious if it were not accurately realized. Miss Taggard obviously will not rest until all but the most inoffensive redundancy is eliminated; her devotion to poetry as an art—an integrity much rarer, in spite of our rehabilitation in technique since 1912, than is usually supposed—will not let her write unevenly. Only with excessive zeal could one discover a single failure in her three volumes of poetry. But it is unfortunately true, on the other hand, that she has not yet produced a single perfect utterance. Quality of expression eludes her. Miss Taggard's poems seem to be written in an unconscious appeal to a quality that continually escapes the terms of her vision. One must account, at any rate, for a perplexing repetition of content and of a certain technical excellence which never quite merge in finality. There is no reason why a poet cannot write many completely different, absolutely realized poems about the same emotions; Miss Taggard simply doesn't.

Her short lyric is her best performance, and it retains enough of its historical properties to be called the epigraphic lyric. It began with the Elizabethans. It was perfected by Landor. Among contemporaries Mr. Yeats alone has been able to give it, in a few examples,

45

the absolute quality beyond competence which takes it out of craft
into art:

> One had a lovely face,
> And two or three had charm,
> But charm and face were in vain
> Because the mountain grass
> Cannot but keep the form
> Where the mountain hare has lain.

And Miss Taggard:

> We will put Time to sleep on that warm hill.
> Lie naked in the tawny grass and fill
> Our veins with golden bubbles.
>   Grass will grow
> Beneath your armpits and between your feet
> Before we take our bodies up, and go
> Like dazzled aliens through the dusty street.

It is impossible to overpraise too highly the deliberate artistry of
these lines; it is equally impossible not to observe the extreme ad-
jectival decoration, which makes the precision of imagery and, at
the same time, diffusion of emotion; it is impossible not to see their
inferiority to the poem by Yeats. The last line of the quotation de-
limits the emotion rhetorically; it is not its realized finality; and
another poem must be sought, both by Miss Taggard and by her
reader.

Considering the limited possibilities of Miss Taggard's chosen form,
one feels that a single volume could have said what is always just
missing utterance in three. Miss Taggard rewrites her poems too
often; more accurately, she attempts to write her one poem. Mr.
Yeats has written only four or five lyrics of the type; his parsimony
is significant. Among the innumerable short lyrics of Landor there
are certainly not more than ten perfect poems; and Landor—with
all respect to Miss Taggard's competence and artistic integrity—was
a better poet than she. "Novelty," says a contemporary critic making the singular demand of poetry that it be creative, "is preferable
to repetition."

From *The Nation* (April 28, 1926)

T. S. Eliot

Poems: 1909–1925, by T. S. Eliot. London: Faber and Gwyer, 1925.

POEMS: *1909–1925* by Mr. T. S. Eliot is a spiritual epilogue to *The Education of Henry Adams*. It represents a return of the Anglo-French colonial idea to its home. A pervasive sense of public duty led Adams into morally and politically active life, but it was not strong enough to submerge the "finer grain," with which his hereditary European culture had endowed him. The conflict was disastrous; he repudiated the American adventure too late. But in Mr. Eliot puritan obligation withdraws into private conscience; a system of conduct becomes a pattern of sensibility; his meagre romanticism, like the artificially constructed ruin of the eighteenth century, is strictly an affair of the past, it has nothing whatever in common with a creed of practical romanticism like that of William James. Going home to Europe, Mr. Eliot has had to understand Europe; he could not quite sufficiently be the European simply to feel that he was there; he has been forced to envisage it with a reminiscent philosophy. And it is not insignificant that the quarterly of which he is the editor is the first British journal which has attempted to relate the British mind to the total European mind; that has attempted a rational synthesis of the traditions of Roman culture; that has, in a word, contemplated order. Mr. Eliot's position in this scheme of recapitulation, of arranging the past when the future seems to him only vaguely to exist, is in some respects particularly fortunate. It has enabled him to bring to England, in his poetry, the sense of a contemporary spiritual crisis, which shell-shock had already rendered acute, but of which the English Channel had perhaps kept out the verbally conscious signification. The essays of Maurras, Valéry,

Massis, the philosophy of Spengler, all may variously attest to the reality of European disorder. It is nevertheless the special poetical creation of Mr. Eliot's cultural disinheritance and gloom.

It has not, I believe, been pointed out that Mr. Eliot's poetry is principally a poetry of ideas, that these ideas have steadily anticipated the attitude of a later essay on the "Function of Criticism." *The Sacred Wood* was written in the years of this anticipatory verse, but this volume is singularly devoid of its chief issues. For the early essays presuppose a static society and the orderly procession of letters: "Tradition and the Individual Talent" presupposes a continuity of traditional culture as literature. The baroque agony of the poetry in the corresponding period was preoccupied, however, with the anarchy which he has subsequently rationalized and for which he has proposed as remedy the régime of a critical dictatorship, in the "Function of Criticism."

The critical idea of disorder began, in the poetry, as the desperate atmosphere of isolation. It was obviously conviction prior to reflection, but to one in Mr. Eliot's spiritual unrest it speedily becomes a protective idea; it ceases to be emotion, personal attitude; one ceases reiterating it as such. This rationalization of attitude puts in a new light the progressive sterilization of his poetry. It partly explains the slenderness of his production: a poetry with the tendency to ideas betrays itself into criticism, as it did in Arnold, when it becomes too explicit, too full. His collected poems is the preparation for a critical philosophy of the present state of European literature. As this criticism becomes articulate, the poetry becomes incoherent. The intellectual conception is now so complete that he suddenly finds there is no symbolism, no expressive correspondence, no poetry, for it. An emotional poetry uncensored by reason would be intolerable to his neo-classical predilections. For Mr. Eliot apprehends his reality with the intellect, and the reality does not yield a coherent theme. This is evidently the formula of *The Waste Land* (1922), where the traditional mythologies are no longer forms of expression, but quite simply an inexplicable burden the meaning of which the vulgar brutality of modern life will not permit the poet to remember. The mythologies disappear altogether in "The Hollow Men" (1925), for this series of lyrics stands at the end of his work as the inevitable reduction to chaos of a poetry of the idea of chaos:

> Here we go round the prickly pear. . . .
> This is the way the world ends
> Not with a bang but a whimper.

The series is substantially an essay on contemporary Europe.

Throughout Mr. Eliot's poetry two principal devices advance the presentation of spiritual disorder. They were previously exploited, the one by Guillaume Apollinaire not later than 1913, the other by André Salmon in 1910. Very little of Mr. Eliot's poetry was written before the latter year. The first is the device of shifted movement, or of logically irrelevant but emotionally significant conclusion, used with typical success at the end of the "Preludes"; I quote from Mr. Malcolm Cowley's unpublished translation of Apollinaire's "Marizibill":

> Through the Hochstrasse of Cologne
> Evenings she used to come and pass
> Offering herself to who would own
> Then tired of walking streets she drank
> All night in evil bars alone. . . .
>
> People I've seen of every sort
> They do not fit their destiny
> Aimless mechanical as wires
> Their hearts yawn open like their doors
> Their eyes are half-extinguished fires.

For the second device, that of projecting simultaneously events which are separated in time, destroying the commonplace categorical perception of time and space and erecting the illusion of chaos—a device of tremendous effect in the Tiresias passage and the Sweeney poems—I quote stanzas from Salmon's "Les Veufs de Rose":

> La duègne a secoué ses jupons
> (Chargez le ciel!—Le herse flambe.)
> Le rat de Hamlet, ce bouffon,
> Vient de passer entre ses jambes.
>
> Chassez le rat, chassez les veufs,
> La vieille fermera la porte,
> Rose enfile le maillot neuf
> D'une soeur rivale enfin morte.

Here is the rhythm of Sweeney, Grishkin, Burbank; also a system of imagery too specific in its properties to have been learned directly from Laforgue, supposedly Mr. Eliot's chief French influence.

While he has all along been under the influence of Laforgue and Corbière, it has not given him his two major effects. From these poets he has borrowed not tricks of construction so much as attitudes and particular lines; for example, Mr. Eliot's beautiful line

Simple and faithless as a smile or shake of the hand—

is a paraphrase, in which the metaphor is made a definite image, of

Simple et sans foi comme un bonjour.

The line was Laforgue's, but now because Eliot has improved it, it is his. And the Elizabethan element is impure. Webster's varied complexity of pattern, its fusion of heterogeneous sensations, breaks down under Mr. Eliot's treatment. It has undoubtedly served him as a model of diction, but the physical presentation of psychological terror and the sense of formal beauty, fused in Webster, are in Eliot, as Mr. Edwin Muir has pointed out, simply mixed, alternately recurring. His Elizabethanism has indubitably been too ingenuously appraised by some critics, and it has thus been objected that such a formula is inadequate to contemporary "problems"; but even were the formula of most of Eliot's poetry what these critics suppose it to be, criticism might as well assert that Dryden was not the poet of his age because he did not permit the lately "discovered" law of gravitation to alter the quality of sensitivity in his verse. Mr. Eliot's poetry has attempted with considerable success to bring back the total sensibility as a constantly available material, deeper and richer in connotations than any substance yielded by the main course of English poetry since the seventeenth century.

He has borrowed intelligently from a great many sources; it is only because of an interested romantic criticism that the privilege has fallen into dishonor. Those aspects of recent French poetry which reappear in Eliot have been impugned as echo and faddism; it is forgotten that some of Massinger's best lines are revisions of Tourneur, are unoriginal. And it is not merely as a skilful borrower that Mr. Eliot is the most traditional poet of the age. For him and for all sound criticism down to Pater the body of literature in the Graeco-Roman culture lives as an organism; he has deliberately employed such of its properties as extend, living, into the creative impulse of his age. His attention in both criticism and poetry has been to the poetry, not to the poet; to the essence and not to the momentary vicar of the essence. The attitude is self-contained, impersonal, classical, and the critics of opportunity and private obsession have regretted the lack of personal exploitation; his unfamiliar system of metaphor has offered a great deal for a vulgar age to misunderstand. His conviction that the traditional inspiration, in immediately inherited forms, is exhausted produced the transition poem, *The Waste Land*: it exhibits this inspiration as it now exists in decay, and it looks by implication toward a new world-order the framework of which Mr. Eliot lacked the excessive divination to supply. He is traditional, but in defining tradition as life, as a living cultural memory, instead of a classical dictionary stocked with literary dei ex machina, he is also the type of contemporary poet.

Mr. Eliot's is a scrupulous, economical mind. It is possible that he has nothing more to say in poetry. "The Hollow Men" ends at least a phase. Whether the difficulty is the personal quality of his puritan culture, as Mr. Edmund Wilson seems to believe, or lies in the tangle of contemporary spiritual forces, it would be hazardous just now to say. But it is evident that he for some reason—like Gray who also lived in a critical transition—cannot "speak out." Arnold's remarks on Gray in this connection are of considerable contemporary interest:

> It [the poetry of his age] was intellectual, argumentative, ingenious . . . not interpretative. Maintaining and fortifying [his mind] with lofty studies, he could not fully educe and enjoy them; the want of a genial atmosphere, the failure of sympathy in his contemporaries, were too great. . . . A man born in 1608 [Milton] could profit by the larger and more poetic scope of the English spirit in the Elizabethan age. . . . Neither Butler nor Gray could flower. They *never spoke out.*

From *The New Republic* (June 30, 1926)

Archibald MacLeish

The Happy Marriage, by Archibald MacLeish. Houghton Mifflin Company, 1924.
The Pot of Earth, by Archibald MacLeish. Houghton Mifflin Company, 1925.
Streets in the Moon, by Archibald MacLeish. Houghton Mifflin Company, 1926.

IN EACH of the last three years Mr. MacLeish has issued a volume of poems. While he has not yet exhibited his power in complete perfection and variety, his work at present yields a clue to an important solution of the contemporary problem. His chief character as a poet is his seriousness, which includes, through the fact of this attitude itself, an intellectual grasp of his position in the contemporary situation. He moves toward the formation of a set of objective values upon which his poetry can lean. The importance of these values, once articulated, will depend upon the degree to which their successive contexts (separate poems) are valid as aesthetic experience.

On the technical side, it is noteworthy that Mr. MacLeish's first volume represents, in its relative spiritual complacency, an aesthetic skepticism. That is to say, Mr. MacLeish in *The Happy Marriage* continued the familiar Meredithian situation with the attempt at universalizing it through merely personal terms. These values were internal to Mr. MacLeish; they never emerged in clean outline in the poems; there was a futility in the nice technique because it erected no stable significances in the end. The realization of this defect must have been the starting-point, the skepsis, of a more fundamental attack upon his problem.

52

The Pot of Earth, however, brings Mr. MacLeish to its center. The framework of this poem is a vegetation myth out of *The Golden Bough*, where the humane properties of the myth are reduced to historical law. The poet's rational intelligence moved in the right direction, in the effort to restore to the myth a *quality* of experience of which the historical method of Frazer had deprived it. He therefore delineated, as a content, as a quality of the myth, definite and unabstract, the sexual growth of a young girl. The poem fails because the myth is for some reason buried too deep in the modern consciousness to be revived with a full sense of its implications: the experiential quality which Mr. MacLeish wished to bestow upon the remote symbol remains external, parallel to the symbol. The poem exhibits once more the dissociated contemporary mind.

Another and more interesting instance of Mr. MacLeish's progress toward objective schematizations is his "Einstein," the most ambitious poem in the third volume. He tries to infer, from the abstractions of Relativity, the qualitative experience which Einstein must have had in formulating them. The poem fails, on the same principle as *The Pot of Earth* fails: the poet does not assimilate the abstractions, and his style is a mixture of scientific restatement and image.

But the lyrics in *Streets in the Moon* represent an enormous advance since *The Happy Marriage*. This can best be explained, I believe, in terms of the author's pursuit of objective, non-psychological values, in *The Pot of Earth* and in "Einstein." The problem involved in these poems shifted his emphasis from the personal emotion conveyed to the pattern of its arrangement, to its framework. Of the fifty-two poems in the book fifteen, in my judgment, are completely successful—an astonishing achievement. We may hope for still greater purity of structure and of diction. For at present the course of Mr. MacLeish's stylistic development lies bare. He is obviously indebted to T. S. Eliot, possibly to Cummings; and undoubtedly to Joyce and Gertrude Stein, who have affected the prose writers of our time and the poets as well.

From *The Nation* (February 16, 1927)

Laura Riding

The Close Chaplet, by Laura Riding Gottschalk. The Adelphi Company, 1926.

THIS VOLUME, the first collection of Miss Gottschalk's* poems, contains thirty-five interesting specimens of her work. If the reader, already familiar with her almost innumerable poems scattered in the course of the last few years through the magazines, find his own preferences not amply represented, he must reflect that Miss Gottschalk will not be held to the narrow bounds of a "first volume." At the outset of a career that must be, in the end, a brilliant success—for Miss Gottschalk, even Miss Gottschalk, performs those emotional revelations which give poetry by women much of its charm, if not its value—at the outset of her career, she has completed a bulk of poetry which a more finical artist might envy at middle age.

Her poems present astonishing successions of wit, irony, mystical vision, and metaphysical insight, and it is difficult to isolate the structural principle of the particular poem. Every poem refers its meaning to the shifting fantasy of sensation which is the personality of the poet; every poem lacks the integral finality of sharp objectivity. And the imaginative push of her lines too often resolves, not into the overtones of the more objective poet, but into mere obscurity. There is at least one exception, however, to this structural deficiency. The most successful poem in the book, "The Quids," is not one of the most distinguished in intention, but it attains to a lucidity and realization which seem to have been made possible by deliberate adherence to a definite limitation in vocabulary and theme.

*Gottschalk was her married name at the time.

54

"The Quids," a metaphysical burlesque, is an essay in romantic wit; its effectiveness is due to the sudden juxtapositions in which the dry terms of the schools, somewhat bewildered, find themselves:

> The quids, that had never done anything before
> But be, be, be, be, be,
> The quids resolved to predicate
> And dissipate in a little grammar.

It is the only modern poem which succeeds with materials supposed, since the Renaissance, to be unpoetical: the cut-and-dried terms of rational systems. It is Miss Gottschalk's distinction, in this poem and in passages of others, to fuse into a single vision all the data of sensibility and thought. It is doutbless true that we are at the beginning of a new era; persons like Miss Gottschalk, Miss Adams, Mr. Hart Crane, and Mr. Archibald MacLeish, perhaps Mr. Read and Mr. Peter Quennell in England, yield the foundations of a school of poetry quite unlike anything in English since the seventeenth century.

It is not surprising, then, that the style of these poets, its mixed vocabulary, its rhetoric, should resemble the Elizabethan. But this style is in no sense pastiche. The similarity is due to similar intention, similar spiritual need. In the Elizabethan age, poetry was the index to culture as a whole, its apex and microcosm. It is quite possible, if poetry shall remain a major art, that it will return to that position. Poetry alone gathers up the discrete departments of the intellect into a humane and living whole. In such passages as these one may see the beginnings of a new attitude:

> Reel to the exile of my face, my face is fair.
> Your lips float down the deaf somnambulism of music,
> Are propelled by a true dream to drop
> Into their unutterable hollow hemisphere. . . .
> After the count of centuries numbers hang
> Heavy over the outnumbered heads and oppress
> The mind one woman has under her dress
> Gasping with chaos and giving out again
> Knowledge like an obsession to the street.

It must be observed, however, that while the distinct points of vision are creative and exact, the supporting structure is not there.

One of the most important new American talents, gifted with the power and material of major poetry, Miss Gottschalk remains—in spite, or perhaps because of, the ambitious reach of her art—blind with the disorder of the age.

From *The New Republic* (March 9, 1927)

John Crowe Ransom

The Gentlemen in Bonds, by John Crowe Ransom. Alfred A. Knopf, 1927.

THE FOURTH volume of John Crowe Ransom's poetry is not the equal in brilliant variety of technical effect or in range of subject-matter of *Chills and Fever*, issued in 1924. But on the whole it is nevertheless the qualitative equal of anything else he has done. And to one who has followed the growth of Mr. Ransom's art from the beginning—a privilege only a few had, and one not so widely coveted, by the method of belated recovery, as it should be—the present collection precipitates the particular essence which is Ransom. The essence is here stripped of the equivocating decoration and virtuosity which have given his art much of its charm yet concealed its chief intentions from all but the most curious and unwearying eyes. It may be, of course, that further additions to the testament complete now with this volume would cry out redundancy—that Mr. Ransom had overwritten himself. However that may be, there would seem to be some profit in the attempt to isolate his motives and qualities, now that they are, from the artistic point of view, fully delineated; and this inquiry entails some comment upon his position in space and time, and upon his origins in that continuum.

In this connection it is worth recalling to mind that certain of Mr. Robert Graves's remarks on Mr. Ransom's English publication, *Grace After Meat*, constitute one of the most astonishing criticisms of American poetry, among many astonishing criticisms, that we have yet heard. Mr. Graves, in effect, announced to the British public that here was a poet giving utterance to the illiterates and poor white of Tennessee, erroneously connecting Mr. Ransom with the Middle West revival then in progress for some years. Involved in Mr. Graves's assertion were two mistakes—a mistake in identifying Ransom's subject-matter (and this it would be impossible to condone even in Professor Phelps) and a mistaken analysis of the quality of intellect controlling and illuminating the material. For Mr. Ransom is the last pure manifestation of the culture of the eighteenth-century South; the moral issues which emerge transfigured in his poetry are the moral issues of his section, class, culture, referred to their simple, fundamental properties. It is a great error to attribute the Southern quality to post-bellum sentimentalism alone, and to repudiate it at its best. The mistake must be charged to that corruption in the critical mind which supposes the vulgar fripperies and superior rudenesses of Mr. James Branch Cabell to be representative of his culture.

Two of Mr. Ransom's qualities in especial connect him with the culture which in its prime registered its genius in politics and law: rationalism and the code of *noblesse oblige.* These qualities, informing every poem, dictate the direction of his artistic vision from all starting-points whatever. Rationalism, not in the sense popularized by the *philosophes,* but in the older and purer sense of the humane tradition, a tradition lying at the very core of the old Southern order, stiffens his poetry with an irony and lucidity, and a subtlety, which elevate it with a unique distinction in the present American scene. His rationalism is the evaluating instrument of the code of honor; it gives the code profundity and edge; it is the weapon of casuistry. The system of casuistry appears in a kind of solemn dandyism, but back of the dandyism lurks a profound stoicism, and an immovable detachment which feeds upon an intellect always sufficient unto itself. All the emotional crises of Mr. Ransom's poems, even of the occasional essays into sheer lyricism like "Vision by Sweetwater," hinge upon the single conviction—*noblesse oblige.* There are, of course, two sides to the medallion; in poems like "The Equilibrists" and "Dead Boy," more vaguely if more subtly in the sonnets "Two Gentlemen in Bonds," Mr. Ransom can render a beautiful commentary upon his tragic personal vision because he accepts the code within which the characters struggle; elsewhere, when he cannot accept their code, as in "Amphibious Crocodile," he pours out the meager yet venomous acid of his satire. In every poem he is either the satirist or the ironist; and as a fine minor artist he has always the same thing to say, in new and unpredictable images.

From *The Nation* (March 30, 1927)

Mark Van Doren

7 P.M. and Other Poems, by Mark Van Doren. Albert and Charles Boni, 1926.

THE POETIC performance of Mr. Mark Van Doren has been steadily limited, but it is neither unpretentious nor slight. He knows his own mind, accepts certain formal limitations, and refuses to amplify his poems beyond the point where their perceptions would perplex his sense of order. Some of his poems, as a matter of course, are less interesting than others. In all of them, however, he knows definitely what he is doing. This quality alone, of poise, of self-direction, would be enough to set him apart as an anomaly among contemporary poets. When the unusual which is not at the same time the novel rears up its head among us, the conspiracy of ignorance settles quietly upon our heads: poetry these days is seldom read with attention. In the case of Mr. Van Doren, the upshot of the anomaly is that he is called an unambitious singer of country matters. It is the opinion of this reviewer that Mr. Van Doren is one of the most ambitious poets now writing, and that the course of his poetry, in two volumes, is a growth in intensity, complexity, and range.

To assign any poetry to its niche in the halls of the literary psychologists is a dangerous, a little presumptuous, and often a meaningless affair; yet it is fairly clear that Mr. Van Doren's poetry appears in terms of the intellect. In the last ten years only the poets who are difficult, or who suffer an inarticulate pessimism, have been described as intellectual. The intellect of W. B. Yeats's later poems has evidently not been consulted. There is no criticism, likewise, for a style like Mr. Van Doren's, which, without having been in the least influenced by Yeats, displays much of the same sort of approach to poetry as Yeats's work since about 1912. The singular smoothness and surface clarity of his verse are due to a rigorous confinement of the material to a definitely conceived and arbitrarily limited plane. The plane is that of ideas, toward which, after careful eliminations, the mixture of experience that the poet must share with other men is gathered up. The elusive quality which his poetry has at its best emerges usually in visual terms, but its effectiveness is due to sudden, almost violent contrasts in image, and Mr. Van Doren, far from being a poet of simple vision, is often the poet of intricate conceits. Take his "Inference," one of the best:

> Who made the evening made the fear
> Of horse and bird and snake and deer;
> Of all that do not learn they live
> Till light itself, grown fugitive,
> Goes breathing by—but turns about,
> And the black pouncer puts it out.
> Then bird and horse and deer and snake
> Go posting home, before they break
> The line that leads them; and their eyes
> Hold all the day that slowly dies.

There is more here than bucolic sincerity of feeling, of which Mr. Van Doren has been frequently accused; there is a deft, consciously sustained technique.

So far is Mr. Van Doren from being the swain of a New England farm that his chief defect as a poet, as I see it, lies in his technical virtuosity. It would be hard to find in this book a single obvious failure. But there are a few unsatisfactory poems. In these there is a certain monotony of rhythm, even when, as in the short quick line, the rhythm is varied. Mr. Van Doren's rhythmical skill occasionally blinds him to the internal direction of the poem itself; we get a poem perfectly rounded out on the surface, but somewhat obscured internally. It is Mr. Van Doren's paradox to be superficially most lucid when he is fundamentally most obscure. The title-poem, in which the last line, simple in itself, is to me on close reading unintelligible, and a poem like "Dilemma," are instances of Mr. Van Doren's occasional weakness for letting the poem get out of hand, and lost under a beautifully organized surface. The poem in this volume which seems to me to be in every respect the most distinguished is "Memories"; it is difficult (the reader should not be drunk, ignorant, or asleep when reading it), but it has none of the structural obscurity of an "easy" poem like "Dilemma." Here the images are not carried forward by the external momentum of the verse; the internal impulse pushes out and finds its own pauses and accents; the rhythms are quite special to the intention of the poem, observing at the same time the definite stanzaic pattern of the lines. In this poem and in passages of others, Mr. Van Doren seems to have found his own equivalent for the later technique of W. B. Yeats. His general outlook and poise, moreover, have much in common with Yeats: he has held consistently to the provincial scene of his childhood, and he remains untouched by the assumptions of the megalopolitan society in which he lives.

From *The Nation* (April 27, 1927)

Phelps Putnam

Trinc, by H. Phelps Putnam. George H. Doran Company, 1927.

THE POETRY of Mr. Phelps Putnam is very well written; he has practised his craft for some years; he has mastered it. Although *Trinc* is a first volume of only seventy-four pages, Mr. Putnam exhibits a maturity and a distinction of style that rank him immediately with the five or six interesting poets who have appeared in the present decade. Putnam not only has the fairly common gift of the poetic phrase, which is frequently only the gift of magazine verse: his poetry is the product of a serious and interesting mind. For this book represents a significant progression from a rich lyricism, enough in itself to get the author a respectable reputation, to a complex symbolism that attempts to organize, in terms of vision, some of the leading philosophical ideas of the age. The progression shows the way in which, with varying materials, the modern poet must go, if he desires to escape from the fashionable attitudes of impressionism and disorder that make up the modern mind.

Trinc is appropriately divided into two sections. The first is lyrical verse by a distinguished talent. Here Mr. Putnam is a lyric poet on the expressive level: there is a great deal of beautiful and original imagery, but there is no framework. There is the unity of tone or mood which is the sum of the images in the poem. The poet cannot exceed emotion, and pass into vision, because he lacks the external framework. The difference is between an imagistic series and a symbolic structure. But on the other hand, the second half of the book is given to the creation of a mythological framework, upon which Putnam elaborates an intricate, and at present fragmentary, vision of contemporary life. The symbols are quite up-to-date. As a counterpart of Hart Crane's "religious gunman" (I wish to suggest no influence whatever passing between Mr. Putnam and Mr. Crane), "Jack Chance" and several other hard-boiled characters become the mythical heroes of a supernatural America.

Of the six poems that disclose the adventures of these heroes, three assume the narrative form, but it is only in the first, "Ballad of a Strange Thing," that anything like pure narration occurs. The style of this poem is simple and discursive; in structure it is extremely complex. It is, in fact, so carefully integrated, that partial quotations are meaningless, and I refrain. From this poem, which is surely one of the most brilliant ever written by an American, Mr. Putnam proceeds, in the others, to elevate his heroes into abstractions. "The Ballad of a Strange Thing" is thus pivotal between the earlier and later styles displayed in the book.

Having transformed his characters, the poet gives up narration and presents the abstract heroes in a kind of timeless vision. The style gets less discursive; it gets more and more oblique; here and there it is obscure. The most interesting poem of this sort—all are of great interest—is "Bill and *Les Enfants Pendus.*" Here Bill Williams, "wandering around" in the scrap-heap and whirl of modern life, comes upon three worthy adventurers:

> Then in the very midst, in Boston, Bill
> Came to a blossoming tree, and thereon hung
> Three young men by the neck and were not dead.
> Before them stood three amphoras of gin
> And in their mouths their words bloomed like the tree.

To match the effect of this passage, one could go to the *Divine Comedy;* it has something of the shock of the question that Guido Cavalcanti's father asks Dante, out of the depths of his flaming coffin:

> Di subito drizzato gridò: Come
> Dicesti: egli ebbe? non viv' egli ancora?
> *No fiere gli occhi suoi lo dolce lome?*

The ingenuity, however, with which Mr. Putnam prepares for these surprises of contrast, results more often in a *nouveau frisson* not unlike that sought after so diligently by the French Romantics. Putnam's lines

> In Springfield, Massachusetts, I devoured
> The mystic, the improbable, the Rose—

are, of course, much nearer Baudelaire than to anything in Dante. The typical instance of the romantic "shudder" is Baudelaire's sudden transition, in "Femmes Damnées," from an impersonal description of perverted sensuality to a dire, equally impersonal vision of its consequences:

> Descendez, descendez, lamentables victimes,
> Descendez le chemin de l'enfer éternal.

Mr. Putnam's verse affords the reader a considerable intellectual interest. His attitude springs, in part, from the current romanticism of the "hard-boiled," the main feature of which is the worship of the crude, the barbaric, the "un-intellectual." Whether the especial prevalence of this attitude among New England writers has any significance for culture, I am not prepared to say. Yet one of the curious things about the present-day revolt against intellectualism is, at any rate, the amount of intellectual ability enlisted in behalf of the *révoltés*—Mr. Putnam's own attitude being a kind of inverted highbrowism. For Putnam's world, wherein the roughnecks, Jack Chance, Bill Williams, and Bigelow Hasbrouck are heroes, is much the same world as that of Dr. Whitehead's metaphysics; or any modern neo-realist world where every position implies every other, and thus ceases to be position—where space abdicates to the event, which is not *in*, but *is* time. Putnam's heroes are symbols of time: they are nowhere, doing everything. They are modern symbols, and his sense of the necessity to bring them into consciousness and order sets him apart as a poet of distinguished intentions; the bare preoccupation with them would mark him as the product of his age.

From *The New Republic* (December 7, 1927)

Yvor Winters

The Bare Hills, by Yvor Winters. The Four Seas Company, 1927.

POEMS BY Mr. Yvor Winters have been appearing for several years in the little magazines, and he has previously published, in pamphlet form, two collections of verse, which acquire a certain interest in the light of the mature style of the present volume. There is always a variety of reasons why certain gifted poets are not immediately taken up. Mr. Winters' case, however, is somewhat special. His poetry occupies an anomalous position, and his limited public fame may be set down to a single cause—the fact that Mr. Winters is starting out as an Imagist some years after the decline of the publicity that accompanied the movement of that name. The circumstance is a little unfortunate for Mr. Winters. But because of the small amount of distinguished verse left by the official Imagists, it is more unfortunate for them.

The Imagist program of the last decade was one of the most ambitious ever made public by a generation of poets. If Mr. Pound were not constitutionally unable to think, it would never have been conceived. Its main idea, which remained negative to the last, was the rejection of a worn-out system of metaphor, with its accompanying patterns of rhythm, that had come down from the nineteenth century. In a sense, of course, the quality of any poetry depends upon the extent to which the poet re-creates his language. But the Imagists were going to make a new language—with a manifesto. They failed. And they failed because language is not merely vocabulary. They failed because a poetry of the image (could it exist) reduces to the parallel exercise of five separate instruments—the five senses—which cannot, without violence done to the first principle of Imagism, be integrated. For Imagism, as it was set forth in the official dogma, contained its own contradiction. It held out for the fresh visualization of objects—that is to say, for the creation of metaphor—but it ignored the total vision, the imagination, by means of which the raw perceptions are bound together into a whole. The Imagists' poetry lacked meaning; though some of their work, the early poems, for example, of Mr. John Gould Fletcher, achieved a kind of success with the merely pictorial and decorative possibilities of the image.

Much of Winters' poetry hobbles along on the necessary limitation of the Imagist technique. But he has cleared up the problem so intelligently that he knows just how far the method will take him; he is perfectly sure; there is no mixed intention. He puts down on the page, in all seriousness, a phrase or a single line, and calls it a poem. Such mistakes betray an intense interest in the properties of the phrase, and the result, in the poems, is a classical precision of statement, a kind of naked elegance, which no other contemporary poet commands:

> dazed and shrill
> the white-lipped boy
> now faces the red sun
> and cries the news.

But Winters does more than the Imagists could do. His poetry rests upon the bare structure of images, but they are arranged so that the "over-statement" usually emerges. This indispensable effect Miss Lowell could seldom manage, and her poetry is rather dry. But Winters keeps the progression of his images quite linear, broken and distinct; while most of the old Imagist poetry was an inert mass of confused sensation. And when the structure of metaphor becomes involved and interwoven, the poet must have the genius for direct and unifying assertion, or the poem will fall apart. Winters has this gift. The poems at the end of the book exceed the Imagist program; the images are involved, piled one upon another. But Winters, to meet the new condition, knows what to do. He binds together the materials of his vision in direct statements. He can go still further in that direction, but at present there is no writing in contemporary poetry more certain of itself, or purer in diction, than the close of "Prayer beside a Lamp":

> The steady courage
> of the humming oil drives back the
> darkness as I drive back sweating death:
> from out a body stricken·by this thought, I
> watch the night grow turgid on the stair—
> I, crumbling, in the crumbling brain of man.

For Mr. Winters sees poetry as a discipline, and his equipment for it is probably, among the men of his decade, the soundest in this country.

From *The New Republic* (March 21, 1928)

Southern Poetry

The Lyric South: An Anthology of Recent Poetry from the South, edited by Addison Hibbard. The Macmillan Company, 1928.

SOME OF THE poems in this anthology are good, others bad; some are accessible, others inacessible elsewhere: the book, in this respect, is like most of its kind. There are the usual distinguished poems by Miss Reese and Miss Roberts, by Mr. Percy, Mr. Davidson and Mr. Ransom. Yet more and more the critical interest in the modern anthology focuses upon the critic's intentions toward the material; less, but not slightingly, upon the material itself. Mr. Hibbard's collection is of the modern variety, which is chiefly an exhibit of the anthologist's poetical doctrine and taste. As such, it will prompt some of his critics to historical considerations.

There were once in this country two nations within the political unity; and although they were supposed to have received the spiritual Union in 1865, the present reviewer dissents, at the risk of being unfashionable, from the belief that the marriage was immediately consummated. It is obvious, rather, that the stringency of the divorce laws was so prohibitive that nullification on the part of the bride was impossible, and that in the end love of finery and good food have made the recalcitrant bride into a wife. The hurried gentlemen who, right after 1865, came southwards (carrying their carpet bags) to administer a "more perfect Union" held some general ideas which their hosts meanly supposed to be related to the benevolence of their economic opinions. Two of the ideas were: (1) Down with sectionalism and local autonomy; and (2) the efficacy of progress. They were the leading ideas in the formation of the Carpetbag South. It is this South in which Mr. Hibbard is interested.

He has two ideas: (1) Down with sectionalism; and (2) up with progress. Southern poets, he says, are conformists in sociology and religion; they are "strangely satisfied with things as they are." Are we to assume that Mr. Hibbard has in the background of this opinion a thorough philosophical view of the purposes of poetry, of the origins of that art, of the conditions under which it is most favorably written? Or are we to understand that he is merely dissatisfied with the Southern scene? Or, again, does he mean that he, as a pedagogue, finds it convenient to teach poetry which contains social ideas, and construes that poetry as deficient which lacks a character easily taught? However this may be, Mr. Hibbard is not hopeless about the progress of poetry in the Southern states. There are, says he, numerous poetry societies, and hundreds of college students are being encouraged to write. Everybody seems to be writing his poems, and Mr. Hibbard seems to have the faith that the quantity of the production is the measure of its success. He seems, moreover, to believe that his book is a "cross-section" of Southern poetry and, as such, an impersonal representation; that other anthologies would contain a "special brief." Mr. Hibbard's two ideas—what shall we say of the critic who uses ideas without knowing it?—his two ideas, applied to the South, make his own collection the most special of briefs: they do not derive from the *milieu* and their application diverts the tendency of his material.

One of his principles of exclusion eliminates poets like John Gould Fletcher, who, conditioned in character and feeling by their native section, have written most of their poetry outside it. Others, who have gone South and reported the physical scene virtually as sightseers, he includes. Yet what else could Mr. Hibbard do? He needed, lacking intimate feeling for his material, some sure and definite sign to go by. A magnolia is unmistakable. I do not assert that Mr. Hibbard's taste is bad; I stop with the regret that he got himself into a difficult position. His attitude, transferred to social intercourse, might exhibit unhappy traits. His anthology plainly tells us that clothes make the man.

The present reviewer is not, as he has already intimated, quite certain that Mr. Hibbard's Introduction is coherent; yet he infers it to be Mr. Hibbard's opinion that the Old Regime (he calls the old manners "foibles") was an error to be charitably reviewed. He deprecates the old order of Colonel Telfair and the "rose of Dixie"—an unexciting act of iconoclasm, since intelligent people in his adopted section have always done it. He assumes, in fact, just enough of the correct attitude to make his mistakes all the more disturbing. Colonel Telfair was ridiculous, but if Mr. Hibbard believes that the Colonel sounded the depths of value in the old provincial society, he has missed the chief meaning of his subject.

If Mr. Hibbard has seen deeply into other poetry, I am at a loss to explain the implied assumption that there is nothing special in Southern poetry to see into. One is tempted to conclude that his difficulty is not merely particular to this subject, but general. The very make-up of the text supports this view. The critic with only slight pretensions to competence knows that a poem about a tree is really about the author's mind. And for this reason poems by the same author ought to be grouped together. If they are to be scattered, the subject headings should have some philosophical exactness, and stand for real divisions in nature or in the mind. A few of Mr. Hibbard's headings are: "People and Portents"; "The Searching Spirit"; "The Fever Called 'Living'"—which will sound literary enough to persons outside literature, but will not stand up to the critical view. For thus a person who has not realized his deficiency in mathematics might confidently assert that the science is made up of three branches severally distinguished by the letters x, y and z. Mr. Hibbard is not very serious.

From the New York *Herald Tribune Books*
(September 16, 1928)

Stephen Vincent Benét

John Brown's Body, by Stephen Vincent Benét. Doubleday, Doran and Company, 1928.

THIS POEM is the most ambitious ever undertaken by an American on an American theme. Yet our judgments must be qualified: there is an important sense in which it is not ambitious enough. There is a sense in which its sole title to poetry is the fact that it is written in verse. It is a weakness of our publishing system that a piece of writing can seldom be sold to the public without having had a great many lies told about it; the author and his work, and the public, too, are put in a false position in which no one, spiritually, is profited. *John Brown's Body* has merit enough; it has hair-raising defects; and yet it deserves to be widely read and, within reason, praised. It is an interesting book, but it is not the kind of work that the public has been led to believe it is.

It has been called among other things an epic and it has been compared, not unfavorably, to the *Iliad*. Mr. Benét himself has no such pretensions; he is modest, and persons who have not lost their heads over the poem should keep them in reviewing the nonsense that has been written about it, lest Mr. Benét be confounded with his prophets and unjustly blamed. The poem is not in any sense an epic; neither is it a philosophical vision of the Civil War; it is a loose, episodic narrative which unfolds a number of related themes in motion-picture flashes. In spite of some literary incompetence in the author and the lack of a controlling imagination, the story gathers suspense as it goes and often attains to power.

Many passages, particularly the lyrical commentaries scattered throughout, are so good that one suspects that the vicious writing, which is most of the poem, comes of too hasty composition. Perhaps Mr. Benét, like most Americans, is mysteriously betrayed into writing with his ear to the ground. It is not his fault; let us say it is the fault of the "system"; yet whoever may be at fault, the poem contains lines like these (which are not the worst):

> Now the scene expands, we must look at the scene as a whole.
> How are the gameboards chalked and the pieces set?

There are too many other lines quite as flat, and they are not all bad because Mr. Benét has a bad ear for verse; they are due, rather, to a lack of concentration in the grasp of the material. The transitions are often arbitrary or forced, and this blemish, which at first sight seems to be merely literary, really takes the measure of Mr. Benét's capacity as a "major poet."

For he does not see the Civil War as a whole. I do not mean that he has not visualized all the campaigns (he has done this admirably), nor that he is deficient in general ideas as to what the war was about. It is simply that his general ideas remain on the intellectual plane; they are disjointed, diffuse, uncoordinated; they never reach any sweeping significance as symbols. The symbol of John Brown becomes an incentive to some misty writing, and instead of sustaining the poem it evaporates in mixed rhetoric. Mr. Benét sees that the meaning of the war is related to the meaning of Brown; yet what is the meaning of Brown? The presentation of Brown as a *character* is interesting; but it is neither here nor there to say, symbolically, that he is a "stone" or, at the end, that the machine-age grows out of his body. It is a pretty conceit, but it is not large enough, it is not sufficiently welded to the subject matter to hold together a poem of fifteen thousand lines. Is it possible that Mr. Benét supposed the poem to be about the Civil War, rather than about his own mind? This would explain its failure of unity; for if a poet have some striking personal vision of life, it will be permanent, and it will give meaning to all the symbols of his irresistible choice. We are permitted to say that the Civil War interests Mr. Benét; it has no meaning for him. He has not been ambitious enough.

Yet Mr. Benét himself appears, in this connection, to have recognized the diffuseness of his impulse. He seems to have felt that the partial glimpses he has given us of the social backgrounds of the war were not strong enough to carry the poem along, and he has contrived a "human interest story" to take the place of a comprehensive symbol. Jack Ellyat, the Union private, is captured at Shiloh; he escapes to a cabin in the woods, where he seduces the beautiful daughter. So far, so good; but when, shortly after the war, the daughter with the baby appears at Ellyat's home-town in Connecticut, the ways of God are not sufficiently mysterious. It is a trick done for effect; the effect is bad.

Many passages in the narrative are complete poems in themselves; a bare collection of these might display Mr. Benét's true stature to better advantage than their context does. Many are distinguished poems; the Invocation is one of the best recent productions by an American.

Mr. Benét has steeped himself in the documents of the age, and many of the historical portraits are freshly done; the interpretation in some instances is highly original. The picture of Lincoln is, as usual, uncritical and unconvincing. The greatest successes are Davis and Lee. If professional historians, particularly those of the Northern tradition, will follow Mr. Benét's Davis, a distorted perspective in American history will soon be straightened out. Nowhere else has Lee been so ably presented, yet the Lee is not so good as the Davis; for, perhaps frightened by the pitfalls, Mr. Benét openly points them out, and the portrait is too argumentative. Yet these and countless minor figures—generals, statesmen, private soldiers, runaway Negroes, plantation ladies, each sharply drawn in his right character—move in an atmosphere all their own that takes us past the literary blemishes to the end. Yet is this atmosphere a quality of the poem or of our memories? Succeeding generations will decide.

From *The Nation* (September 19, 1928)

Mark Van Doren

Now the Sky and Other Poems, by Mark Van Doren. Albert and Charles Boni, 1928.

THIS IS Mr. Van Doren's third volume of poetry, and it is one of the half-dozen really distinguished books of poetry that have appeared in America in the last ten years. His performance has exhibited, from the outset, a continuity of impulse, a certainty of direction, and consequently a homogeneous development of style. There are other contemporary poetic minds as interesting as Mr. Van Doren's, but none knows itself so well. He is that rare American poet who has been able to sustain, over a number of years, a single purpose, and to extend and deepen this purpose without doing violence to his style as it was originally conceived. Marianne Moore and Wallace Stevens, of Van Doren's generation, alone have equaled him in the certainty of their craft; but their impulse contrasted with his (which is complex and dynamic) is simple and static, and easier to control.

Mr. Van Doren is, in fact, if not the most brilliant stylist of our time, one of the most accomplished craftsmen. It would be difficult to find in all his work an ill-written poem. There are, however, several unsatisfactory poems. There has always been in his verse, as I have previously pointed out, an occasional obscurity which appears when the poem seems, at first glance, to be simplest and clearest. Take this stanza, from one of the "Philosopher's Love Songs":

> I learn at last
> To wait alone.
> She is my own
> And tethered fast—

But to no mast
And to no moan.

It is an image that puts the seal of logical meaning upon the poem
but which leaves the emotion diffuse. This kind of obscurity, in a
poet of Van Doren's stature, is due to a gift for writing which persists
at those times when the impulse is diffuse or repetitive. But this
analysis, in the light of his most recent poems, requires extension:
the symbols that first occupied his mind were not equal to the full
reach of his vision, and while these early symbols could not com-
prehend all that he had to say and left his emotion diffuse, his skill
as a rhetorician saved him from the appearance of failure.

Certain minute changes in natural scenes are the source of Van
Doren's early symbolism, and in the best poems the correspondence
between the feeling and the image is so exact that it has tempted
him to attribute philosophical value to the "objective reference" of
his feeling—that is, to nature itself. There has therefore been latent
in his impulse the tendency to document his sense of nature to the
fullest. But he has always had more than the sense of nature, or at
any rate a sense quite different from that. Only those poems in which
the feeling is intimately related to the natural symbol are completely successful. Nature, in short, has been the sustaining framework of Van Doren's best work up to the present time. But it has
not exhausted his vision; there has been a certain number of poems,
written in the effort to document the sense of nature, which contain
traces of an impulse alien to that intention. What to do with this
alien impulse and what its significance is in relation to the original
one are questions that landed Mr. Van Doren in a serious dilemma.

But, as a conscious artist, he has, in the present volume, analyzed
his predicament, and he sets about correcting the divided emphasis
of his past work. Nature, he says, in a long history of his mind entitled "We Come Too Late," no longer sustains him: the last poem
in the book predicts a more varied background for his future work.
There is, indeed, at present interesting evidence of this.

There are few poets whom the sense of nature has supported
throughout a long career, and there is nothing peculiarly modern in
Mr. Van Doren's rejection of an early belief. That he has, however,
been able to extricate himself from a predicament that would de-

stroy most poets and to use the predicament itself as a fresh starting-point attests to the vigilance of one of the most acute intelligences in contemporary poetry.

Yet, if there is nothing specifically modern in a rejection of nature, the positive direction with which Van Doren follows his rejection puts upon it a definitely modern interpretation. It is not that his feeling for nature has weakened; it is rather that he can no longer believe in it as a realm of fixed symbols adequate to what he has to say. It no longer has the intrinsic value that he once thought it had. As a modern mind he has been affected by the scientific version of nature (or by its moral equivalent in the social atmosphere), which has killed its human values. Turning away, he finds that the only values accessible to him as a modern lie within himself. And so, breaking off from the early tendency toward a minute documentation of the sense of nature—possible only so long as nature has intrinsic human values—he grows more and more interested in the creation of intricate and elusive emotions, which a simple inspection of the face of nature would not support. Poems like "Tiresias," "The Disguise," "Civil War," in which the imagery is composed of irrational symbols irreducible to the logic of prose, connect Van Doren with his contemporaries Wallace Stevens, Phelps Putnam, Hart Crane. There is, in these recent poems, a quality not unlike that of the symbolist poets. And there is, besides, a quality of macabre ferocity in some of his images unlike anything he has done before and unlike anything by anybody else. Here is a specimen from "Civil War":

> In the forbidden country where the sod
> Grows down and down, with restless blue roots, gray roots,
> In the dark windy land no one can leave,
> Separate necks yearn homeward;
> Separate hungry shoulders pull and pull.
> *Wind, oh wind, I did not come to stay;*
> *I must be there tomorrow, not to miss. . . .*
> But the dark wind is earless, and the day
> Is endless, and the grasses hiss and hiss.

> From *The Nation* (December 19, 1928)

American Poetry Since 1920

SHORTLY AFTER 1920 a popular agitation for poetry, the most successful and sensational in our history, came to a close. Between 1912 and 1918 several distinct movements had got under way, and isolated poets, like Robinson and Frost, who might otherwise have come less swiftly to fame, were taken up on the rising sea of that time and were soon riding the full crest of the wave. There were doubtless certain defects in the intellectual climate of that decade, and yet it appeared to have a singular virtue—that of providing an atmosphere through which poetry could be readily communicated to the public. This atmosphere had quickly spread over the Northern section of the political unit (the South at that time had not yet risen to speech), and it seemed as if poetry had at last reached the public as intimately as the nineteenth century Bostonians had made their own poetry reach themselves. Then, suddenly, the genie withdrew into his bottle. He left the air as pellucidly thin as he had found it. And the poets, breathing heavily, burrowed once more into their holes.

The defect of the time was the fact that the air the poets breathed was not their own, but the breath of the genii (for there were two): Miss Amy Lowell and Mr. Louis Untermeyer. Miss Lowell's talent for being a popular figure had convinced the public, for a time, that it was interested in poetry; and yet, even before her death, she had lost much of her hold upon the popular imagination. This may or may not have been due to the ingratitude of the public, which refused its attention to her ideas after it had ceased to be amused. At any rate, by 1920 Imagism had played out, and polyphonic prose, no longer controversial, was no longer read.

Mr. Untermeyer's position was different. He pinned his faith to no single movement, but with amazing success applied an elastic spirit to the comprehension of them all. He was able to phrase the right public interpretation of a great many poets: Sara Teasdale, E. A. Robinson, Robert Frost, Carl Sandburg . . . but the list is inexhaustible. Yet, in the last six or seven years, his influence has perceptibly declined. Mr. Untermeyer, taking always great risks, has made mistakes; but the very decline of his influence attests to the integrity of a useful career. He is temperamentally a partisan critic; his heart has always been with the poets of his own generation; and his service consists in his having stamped their reputations upon the mind of the reading public. Only critics of the first order can bridge two generations and outlast the enthusiasms of their own time. Mr. Untermeyer leaves no successor, and the popular defense of poetry has lost its effectiveness. The public has been left to infer that poetry itself has declined. Already there were giants in those days.

But, as a matter of fact, American poetry is now in certain respects more interesting than it has ever been. Its range of feeling is wider, its technical resources are deeper—its intention, in fact, is better informed than that of any other poetry in our literature. The contrast of its motives with those of the preceding generation will make them clear.

The poets who made the second decade of this century famous as the American Renaissance exhibited, in spite of their local differences, a singleness of outlook that seemed to prove that we had, after all, a national spirit and that our period of servitude to foreign models had ended. But, just as the atmosphere of communication between poet and public was misleading, there was something misleading in the unified Americanism of their attitude: it was not all that it seemed to be. With the exceptions of Robinson and Frost, the leading figures came from the Middle West. The spirit of that region was boomed much as its land had been two generations before. Lindsay and Sandburg and Masters tracked down the local character of their section, and, once found, it easily fitted, under the pressure of frontier optimism, into the framework of national types and heroes who seemed to speak for the whole country. But the intention of these poets towards their material turned out to be only mildly representative, their production a kind of hurried programme music. What emerged was America boomed in terms of the West.

How successfully this movement made itself out to be the spirit of a united America is measured by the mistake of an English critic writing about John Crowe Ransom: Mr. Robert Graves assumed that, as an American poet, Mr. Ransom (who came after Sandburg and has a different background) was attempting to "express" the poor whites of the South. Mr. Graves had been instructed by *The Spoon River Anthology*; but the significance of his error will be clearer in a moment.

The misleading quality of the Middle-Western poetry boom came directly out of the conception of poetry that lay back of it. This was simple, untutored, and crude. And its production had the features of a hasty revolt. Moody, Woodberry, and Miss Peabody were decadents; they were severely inoculated against the living American scene. But the revolt from them was really carried out on their own plane of vision: their diction was broken up and a fresher idiom substituted; the physical scene was noted in more vivid detail. But the intensity of vision was not increased, and after the spell of the American catchwords had subsided, chaos yawned vastly as before. Beneath the aggressive Americanism of Sandburg, Lindsay, Masters, there was not a profound ordering of experience, personal or common; it is not surprising that they failed to give us a mature style. What they gave us was, in the end, *News from the West*. And Miss Lowell and Mr. Untermeyer were not unwilling to publish it.

The important thing, then, to remember, so far as the new poets are concerned, is the failure of their predecessors to leave them firm ground to stand upon. The sociological excitement of the preceding generation was not disciplined; it yielded no permanent values. The excitement has abated; the new poets have not been able to share it, for it was not strong enough to make a tradition; and they have had to begin over again. Their performance is thus more varied, and it lacks the sustaining force of a common idea. It lacks utterly the belief in a united America. The poets of our own time have not been able to organize a school that could advertise itself as representative of the whole country.

There have, of course, been groups, like the Fugitives of Tennessee who did not advertise themselves at all. These poets started with open minds—that is, with the simple aim of writing poetry. But after five or six years it became clear that quite unconsciously they were fostering a sectional spirit, that they were indifferent to the Middle Western procedure of rendering an American as distinguished from any other scene, and that finally they were all private persons trying to solve the esthetic problem each in his own way. They were willing to draw upon all the resources of poetry that they knew, for it was obvious that their sectionalism, if it existed, and their nationalism, if that existed, would take care of themselves. There was no attempt to force the materials at hand into an easy significance (the mistake of the South Carolina poets). Fugitive poetry turned out to be profoundly sectional in that it was supported by the prejudices, feelings, values, into which the poets were born. Because the approach of the Fugitives to their art was the normal one, and because the normal attitude has been absent in America for several generations, the history of the Fugitive group is not an unprofitable study.

The significance of Mr. Graves's mistake regarding Mr. Ransom's intentions now becomes clear, and it illuminates the break between two generations of American poets. Far from booming the conspicuous properties, physical and social, of their native scene, John Crowe Ransom, Donald Davidson, and the other Fugitive poets took, in these properties, only that minimum of public interest that one feels in one's arms and legs. Their original approach to poetry was therefore pure—that of craftsmen. I hesitate to describe this approach as esthetic, for the term is debased. The chief emphasis was laid, or, more strictly, was discovered to have been laid, upon form and style.

This is the leading characteristic of the best poetry written in all sections of America since the era of *The Spoon River Anthology*. The motives of a generation of poets, seen through a reducing-glass, are the motives of the Fugitive group. This group had little or no influence upon the poets outside the South. They began writing in 1921, and their work points in a direction that poets everywhere, at that time, felt bound to take.

The collapse of the Middle Western movement left the younger poets helplessly open to conviction, and the recent preoccupation with form and style is largely due to, has been largely organized under, the influence of Ezra Pound and T. S. Eliot. This influence has concentrated the energy of a generation. It has been on the whole beneficial. The best talents have recovered from the direct imitation of their masters, so that the present generation can offer to the public six or seven poets who in the art of writing are superior to the best (Mr. Robinson being excepted) of the preceding generation. I need only to name Mark Van Doren, John Crowe Ransom, Hart Crane, Léonie Adams, Yvor Winters, Archibald MacLeish; there are others almost as good.

The pursuit of form and style I have called a "direction," and it has been cherished as such by isolated persons and groups, notably the *Secession* writers, now scattered and reformed, and the recent Chicago school composed of Samuel Putnam, Mark Turbyfill, and, for a time, Glenway Wescott and Yvor Winters. But it is quite obvious that the most efficient piece of machinery is incapable of charting its own course: the stylistic excellence of contemporary American poetry is equalled only by the variety in the chaos that it holds up to the view. In this chaos there are several different Americas, none of which contains all the values of the whole and which, with respect to the whole, represents disorder. But the degree to which individual poets have achieved a triumph over a limited material is greater than that achieved by the preceding generation envisaging a more comprehensive surface.

The inference to be drawn from this distinction is irresistible. The experiment that tried to find values for the whole of the American scene succeeded in erecting a set of fictions which collapsed after a short period of excitement; these fictive values have declined because they did not proceed from an intense realization of the projected material. They were forced, but *not made good*. The new poets steadily refuse to issue a special plea for any set of current values. They are trying to write poetry, and they are succeeding in integrating as much value as they find in themselves or in their associations with some limited scene. Mr. Phelps Putnam, from Massachusetts, and Mr. Robert Penn Warren, from Kentucky, have as much in common as a French poet and an English poet writing in the same age: only a big word, like *Zeitgeist*, can establish their communication. We must infer, then, that the attempt to boom America as a unity of feeling has failed, and that the unity has, at cock-crow, limped off a vague and ghostly abstraction, for which no one seems bent upon finding a definite symbol. For the new poets are concerned with personal and local symbols, and their poetry tends towards provincialism.

This, then, is the direction of modern poetry in America. Yet such a direction is, at least for the moment, quite negative: the literary provincialism of the younger poets has, unluckily, no political connections, and, more unluckily still, the only temporo-spatial support it can hope to find lies in a group of moribund cultures. A survey, therefore, of the accomplishment of the new generation brings out a perplexing variety of impulses. In the South there is the attempt to define the past in terms of an unsympathetic reaction to the industrial era; the poets in that region are conservative with respect to their own traditions, but they are prepared to use all the methods associated in the popular mind with literary "radicalism". The Middle West, since the time of Lindsay and Masters, has repudiated its interest in the local speech and scene; the short memory and vague future of that section have easily plunged the young writers into "abstractionism" and anti-intellectualism in extreme forms, such as the poetic impostures (deliberate or not) of Samuel Putnam and Mark Turbyfill; but this tendency indicates a genuine impulse, which motivates the distinguished poetry of Hart Crane. The state of the New England mind is (as usual) less simple; it is still, in spite of much internal cleavage and some external disguise, a single mind, of which Putnam and Cummings are only different facets. Cummings is a deeply moral sensibility without moral ideas—a predicament which induces him to exaggerate the value of his perceptions and makes him too often the showman. Putnam is a showman too: he is a New England divine who, on the emotional plane, stands by his tradition (there is something of Robinson's feeling in him), but who appears to reject it in his concern with spectacular modern symbols; his impulse runs true to form in his mystical and romantic quest of God—as distinguished from the common-sense rationalism of the quest of the good life on the part of his Southern contemporaries. New England, the South, the Middle West, these are still our resources, and they remain distinctive if not intact. And there is the far West, where Robinson Jeffers stands alone. Jeffers's gift for narrative is unequalled in England or America, and he has invented a new narrative style. He represents, with his symbols of inversion and sterility, with his anti-intellectualism, the most ambitious reach of the West to erect its disorder and rootless energy into a symbol of the whole American scene.

A certain quality of excellence, it must be said, is the sole connection between a great number of very different poets. John Crowe Ransom has published three books of verse. The first, *Poems About God* (1919), was experimental; it barely foreshadowed the distinctive quality for which this poet is now famous. *Chills and Fever* (1924) and *Two Gentlemen in Bonds* (1927) evince the perfect fusion between style and attitude. Ransom's poetry is a richly fulfilled moment of vision which seems to be incapable of growth and change; but his intellectual resourcefulness permits us to expect a later performance that will be quite different from anything he has done. The poetry of Donald Davidson, like Ransom's, leans heavily upon the rural culture of his section; only Davidson's method of dealing with local values, since the appearance of *An Outland Piper* (1924), grows more and more historical; *The Tall Men* (1927) is a kind of subjective epic which takes a single attitude from the pioneer period through the Great War. This interesting poem is brilliantly and incoherently written. Mark Van Doren is in some respects our most perfect craftsman. He found, in his first volume, *Spring Thunder* (1924), a style which, in two successive books, has been modified and extended, without being changed, until it is now equal to the demands of a highly complex vision. The surface simplicity of Van Doren's first poems was misleading: he is one of the most profound sensibilities in America. In his third volume, *Now the Sky* (1928), he begins the development of a complex symbolism. Léonie Adams and Louise Bogan have each published a single distinguished volume. Miss Bogan's *Body of This Death* (1923), a slight but almost perfect exhibit, announced the most accomplished woman poet of the time: Miss Bogan had succeeded in reducing a sharp sense of peripheral sensations, to which women are peculiarly sensitive, to form. But Miss Adams's *Those Not Elect* (1925) heralded a close rival. Miss Adams's range is, in fact, considerably greater than Miss Bogan's, and her style is richer and more mature; her mind is probably the freest in contemporary poetry; it is susceptible to release by all the experience at her command. Her style is a little too heavily burdened with a superabundance of imagery, and her poems often conceal their central ideas; this defect of composition may be corrected in time.

Marianne Moore and Wallace Stevens, different as they are from each other, have in common certain elements of style: precision of statement, decorative imagery, and a sense of the allusive value of nonsense phrases. The intention of Miss Moore's *Observations* (1924) is slight, but its technical perfection has not been surpassed by a contemporary writer. She is a Victorian in whom Victorian convictions are lacking, but in whom the habits of feeling which correspond to those convictions remain; she is, in fact, deficient in compulsions of any sort—that is to say, in "ideas"; and her verse proceeds from a perceptive mechanism which seems to run on its own momentum. Stevens is quite differently motivated. *Harmonium* (1923) contains an impulse more serious than Miss Moore's. His dandyism, which has been ably described by Mr. Gorham B. Munson, is the perfect surface beneath which plays an intense Puritanism. He is undoubtedly the most finished poet of the age, and he is the only American poet who has been intelligently affected by the Parnassians and the Symbolists.

There remain three important craftsmen. Hart Crane's one volume, *White Buildings* (1926), is probably the most distinguished first book ever issued in the country. It has been followed, in the last two years in various journals, by fragments of an American epic to be entitled *The Bridge*: Crane is the only interesting talent of his generation who is preoccupied with the idea of united America, and it is worth pointing out, again, that he comes from the Middle West. His chief defect is the lack of a system of disciplined values which would clarify and control the most prodigal poetic gift in America. His genius for sheer writing—for composition, for variety and subtlety of rhythm, for freshness of imagery—occasionally gets out of hand: his literary talent exceeds at the moment what he has coherently to say. Crane's blank verse is one of the few important contributions made by a contemporary to poetic style. Archibald MacLeish continues to promise more than he has achieved. His literary competence is tremendous. His writing has an inveterate distinction, but it lacks direction, weight, and solidity; there seems to be no leading symbol that plays upon his ideas and he has thus not been able to develop a consistent style. Yvor Winters is in the experimental stage. *The Bare Hills* (1927) brings to an end his first phase; this book, had it appeared ten years ago, would have won its author the first place among the Imagist poets.

There are certain other poets whose work has not been published in books, but it is so good that it should be better known. Edmund Wilson has written some of the most accomplished poetry of our time. In attitude and the sense of value he belongs less to the generation of Crane and MacLeish than to the society that produced Mr. John Jay Chapman: his poetry is almost exclusively concerned with social appearances and their meaning, and he has a good deal in common with the author of *London* and *The Vanity of Human Wishes*. Malcolm Cowley has published in the last few years very little poetry; he is one of the most finished writers in America. He was deeply affected by post-bellum literary movements in France, and under this influence he wrote a good deal of verse, which is not his best. Cowley is one of those rare American poets genuinely gifted with rural and regional feeling, and his best poetry is motivated by it. Robert Penn Warren, a member of the Fugitive group, is shaking off, in recent poems, the influence of T. S. Eliot; his best verse, like Cowley's, derives its symbols from a specific region; but, unlike Cowley's, it is supported by certain moral obsessions that give it intensity and depth. There are other interesting poets—Saville Clark, Lincoln Fitzell, Margaret Moore, Janet Lewis, Merrill Moore—who may be expected to produce interesting verse. So little, however, of the work of these poets is accessible that it is difficult to predict their future.

The conclusion to which the impartial observer of the American scene is driven is that there is no homogeneous body of beliefs and feelings into which the poet may be educated; in all these poets there is no positive attitude that we may describe as national, as peculiarly our own. The formation of such an attitude is, in a sense not easily defined, the American problem. But it is significant that the only poet of the new generation—as I have already observed—who is attempting to create such an attitude in national terms should come from the Middle West. This is the section where local tradition is weakest; the spiritual well-being of the West depends upon its success in assimilating the cultural tradition of the older sections. I have pointed out the failure of the past generation to achieve this unity of feeling. Hart Crane's effort in this direction is more ambitious than Lindsay's or Sandburg's, and because he is a poet of the first order the publication of *The Bridge* will be an important event in contemporary letters. Of its success in creating a national myth it is our privilege to be sceptical in advance.

For the American problem, as I have stated it, is not national at all; it is sectional. It is the problem of survival in the Middle West. The Middle West, of course, is not purely a geographical term; it applies to any community where the population is restless and its activities industrialized. And it is not surprising that there is a powerful metropolitan school of writers who have undertaken the formation of the American idea: New York absorbs and intensifies the motives of all our Middle Wests. This motive is, in general, disorder attempting to correct itself by means of the further disorder of catchwords and slogans. There is no reason to infer, from the distress into which the lack of an American myth betrays us, that it is possible to create one. It is not even desirable that such a myth should be created. The only effective procedure in the present crisis has been, surprisingly enough, described in *The New Republic* by Mr. Waldo Frank. (I say it is surprising that Mr. Frank should describe it because he is himself the product of the megalopolitan life that has undone us.)

This procedure is the formation of groups. Our groups since the middle of the nineteenth century have been rootless collections of people spellbound by Utopia or advancing some special plea. It is hard to find a disinterested group in our recent history. The Imagists were not a genuine group; they were a miscellany of people who, under Miss Lowell, formulated a public cry. Other groups, like the recent "Secessionists", have formed to resist the organized literary journalism of New York. It is outside the purpose of this essay to analyze the intention of the powerful group headed by Mr. A. R. Orage, which exhibits the fallacy of most of our groups. For external authority which does not work up through the terms of American life only cuts its adherents away from their roots, and thus accelerates the process of disorder which it proposes to correct.

The group should be provincial. Its formation should be accidental. Its activity should be, not the circulation of opinion, but the discipline of art forms. It should be a group of craftsmen—of painters, of philosophers, of poets. It is possible that never again will powerful groups, so motivated, appear in the United States. And yet the present state of American poetry points to certain negative conditions favorable to their appearance.

For the disordered spirit of the new poets is collective; as individuals they have attained to a more intense personal ordering of the spirit than their immediate predecessors had achieved. They lack the facile optimism of the past generation and evince but little feeling for solidarity in modern life. The poets have retired upon their private resources. The possibility of more limited solidarities has increased. The personal resources of the poet are capable of further intensification if they can be brought back to contact with the local cultures from which, in each instance, they originally sprang. Only a return to the provinces, to the small, self-contained centres of life, will put the all-destroying abstraction, America, safely to rest.

The rootless character of contemporary life explains the tenuous substance which informs the mind of the contemporary poet. It explains the obscurity and difficulty of his verse. There are no fixed points in the firmament, no settled ideas of conscience, which he can call upon to simplify his speech. He lacks ideas, but it is not his business to make them; it is his business to put them to use.

It is a great error to suppose that modern poetry is intellectual. It is anti-intellectual: the type of intellectual poet is Alexander Pope, who dealt almost exclusively with ideas. To tell the contemporary American poet that he is an intellectualist is to obscure the difficulty of his problem in his own mind, and to give him a false sense of security.

From *The Bookman* (January, 1929)

Malcolm Cowley

Blue Juniata: Poems, by Malcolm Cowley. Harrison Smith and Jonathan Cape, 1929.

THIS COLLECTION of fifty-five poems covers the history of Mr. Cowley's mind in the last ten years. Like all of his writing, it is beautifully finished, and as poetry it is of an order very rare in the American scene: Mr. Cowley not only has a specific talent for poetry, he is a highly trained man of letters, and his verse is a fine example of the discipline of craftsmanship that few Americans achieve. Between the generation of Chapman and Brownell and the generation of Cowley there were few Americans who successfully cultivated more than one type of literature. Cowley has done almost every kind of writing, and done it well. This is his first book, and it corrects one's previous belief that the finely ordered surface of his style was somewhat deficient in coherence and depth. No American at present writes a more lucid prose than Cowley, and yet it is now clear that prose, certainly critical prose, is not his true medium. His mind is basically concrete and unspeculative; he brings to facts and observations an even, emotional tone that is the mark of a genuine style; but in criticism Cowley's instinct for exact definition is not strong; and the necessity for a certain amount of abstraction only violates the even tone of his style. It is in poetry, at least for the present, that Mr. Cowley may be seen at his best.

And yet the long discipline of prose has given to his poetry much of its distinction of form. If Cowley might have written better, or at least as well, in another age, that age is the early eighteenth century. His poetry has gone diligently to the school of prose: there is hardly

a passage in this book that is not good prose before it is good poetry—a merit that not much contemporary poetry may claim:

> Between the waves, out of the sight of land
> at night toward an unseen beacon swimming
> the sea flung her arms about his arms
> in foam, mingled her hair with his
> and clung against his breast
> against his lips the salt pulse of the sea.

These lines from "Leander," one of his finest poems, move with the
loose orderliness of highly conscious prose—without any falling off
in the poetry.

Mr. Cowley has arranged his poems in two ways, and the grouping
is of two kinds. There are poems belonging to a certain year, or to a
period of two or three years; there are poems belonging to a sentiment or an idea which come under distinct headings. The latter are
his best work; but the former extend and enrich the book as a whole,
and give it important documentary interest. The value of *Blue Juniata* as poetry is high; as a document of the first post-war generation
it is unique. (The sections of the book are welded together and placed
in the time when the poet wrote them, by short prose paragraphs
written with great point and skill.) Cowley's generation appeared
after the war had given the "genteel tradition" and the provincial
ways of life in America a staggering blow. This volume is the record
kept by a member of this generation who broke with his past, witnessed the moral collapse of Europe, and returned to make the best
of the confused intellectual life of post-war New York.

There are particular scenes and emotions that linger in Cowley's
imagination: his book is well named for a river in Pennsylvania by
which, I believe, he spent his childhood. Out of this material he has
written his best poems. His regional verse is superficially less brilliant than the poems he wrote in direct contact with Europe, and
less striking technically than certain abstract poems ("Death,"
"Time," "William Wilson"); but it is far more moving, less self-
conscious; his technical resources are used to better effect, if less
spectacularly. An inferior artist like Mr. Vachel Lindsay, or even a
superior one like Mr. Frost outside his best moments, would have
boomed the local features of the Juniata country, and given us more

Juniata than poetry. Mr. Cowley, however, refuses to publish pretty landscapes and characters without first reducing them to order and form. It is this almost unerring sense of form that gives value to the slightest pieces in this volume.

There are no bad poems in the book: the difference between his best and his worst does not lie in the difference between good and bad writing. This fact defines, for the moment, Mr. Cowley's talent. In him we see neither the failure of careless writing nor the grand failures of Blake or Hardy; for although he is a romantic poet—that is, a poet dealing with sentiments and passive emotions rather than with obsessive ideas that are driven to the point of disintegration (Shakespeare, Racine)—he stops his impulse on the hither side of order; he does not push it over the line dividing incoherence from intelligible form. There are no great moments in Cowley, and there are no disconcerting lapses. There is subdued emotion; there are exact feelings and images; and over all, a subtle vision of the startling qualities of common things. Malcolm Cowley is one of our most distinguished talents, and he has given us, in an unrhymed lyric "The Urn," a poem the quality of which is, within its range, unsurpassed in our time:

> Wanderers outside the gates, in hollow
> landscapes without memory, we carry
> each of us an urn of native soil
> of not impalpable dust a double handful
>
> carelessly gathered (was it garden mould
> or wood-soil fresh with hemlock needles, pine
> and princess pine, this little earth we bore
> in secret, vainly, over the frontier?)
>
> A parcel of soil not wide enough
> or firm enough to build a dwelling on
> or deep enough to dig a grave, but cool
> and sweet enough to sink the nostrils in
> and find the smell of home, or in the ears
> rumors of home like oceans in a shell.

From *The New Republic* (August 28, 1929)

Rolfe Humphries

Europa, and Other Poems and Sonnets, by Rolfe Humphries. New York: Crosby Gaige. Limited Edition, 350 copies, printed in Holland, 1929.

MR. HUMPHRIES' is not the kind of verse that excites the public: the poet successfully conceals, perhaps deliberately, his personality. There is no dramatizing of his own life; he is not concerned to let us know that he is living one. It is a poetry of delicate, sometimes diffused and sometimes controlled perception. The theme is usually abstract, impersonal—death, impermanence—or some trivial incident that illuminates the abstract theme. So much for his chance with the public. As for the poets, they will not be able to learn anything from Humphries, for he writes easily in a manner comfortable for him; but this manner is not a style. Its character is too unfixed. Take these lines on a passionate woman:

> Pity her, poor automaton!
> It cannot be so very good
> To fall in love with flesh and blood
> And have it clearly understood
> That one is permanently wood.

Mr. Humphries' manner is, of course, the most difficult of all to elevate into a style. It is not personally expressive; it is impersonal, and it is made up of common words; it tends to lie flat unless considerable skill is exercised in arranging climaxes and overtones. The following lines, by another poet, begin as flatly as anything in Humphries; but observe the sudden climax at the end, the almost imperceptible transition from flat words to rhetorical splendor, without violating the even tone of the *manner* which is a quality underlying the passage and holding it together, and distinct from the stylistic effect:

> The pleasant whining of a mandoline
> A clatter and a chatter from within
> Where fishmen lounge at noon—
> Where the walls of Magnus Martyr hold
> Inexplicable splendor of Ionian white and gold.

Mr. Humphries has manner and tone, but not style.

For this reason, I believe, the best poems out of thirty-four collected here are the sixteen sonnets. There are excellent passages in the miscellaneous work, but on the whole the poems are a little diffuse; they do not quite come off in the end. The sonnets, however, are almost invariably, but within Humphries' limits, successful. The writing is much more compact; the images more certain; the poem is rounded off, complete. Here is the sestet from "Homo Additus Naturae"—a title reminding us that Humphries is an excellent Latinist:

> Some day a ragged, curious old man
> Will come and sun his reminiscent bones,
> Hungry to keep what permanence he can,
> The potent trees, the dull magnetic stones,
> Still unaware how cunningly they drew
> Him into them, long since, when he was you.

The reason for his greater success with the sonnet seems to lie in the conventional demands of that form. He takes a single idea; exposes it in the octet; resolves its meaning in the sestet. It becomes a kind of conceit which Humphries with great delicacy plays upon. The fixed character of the sonnet form permits this, and helps him to avoid the diffuseness of his work in the freer forms. For the flatness of his manner is, perhaps, due to a lack of emotional intensity, and he requires the conceit to give it point. In each sonnet we get, instead of concentrated feeling, surprise.

From *The New Republic* (February 19, 1930)

American Poetry

Our Singing Strength: An Outline of American Poetry (1620–1930), by Alfred Kreymborg. Coward-McCann, 1930.

MR. KREYMBORG'S pretensions to criticism are so modest and his industry is so great; his kindness to American poets, dead and living, particularly the living, even including myself, is so conspicuous and unwearying, that one puts down his book with the belief that one should be disarmed of a sense of its limitations and even of its downright faults. The book is overwhelmingly, on every page, a labor of love. The author says: "If a lover is one who must spread his affection broadcast, then the present student is one. My feeling for American poetry dominates my life. . . . It is not enough that I feel this way. One must have comrades." And he would have them, if critics were not unregenerate; Mr. Kreymborg's "Preliminary Confession" is enough to deprive one of one's last weapon: he appeals, from the barbaric confusion of New York, for a comradeship among writers—an appeal to which, I admit with regret, I am almost totally deaf. For the other side of the appeal is a "faith" in poetry, so sincere, so irrational and so vague as to throw this reviewer into a state of alarm—a faith that leads the author to make the history of American poetry over into the history of a religion. It is only proper that a critic should be mastered by his subject, but not to the degree of succumbing to it.

Only 252 of the 643 pages are given to the poets who precede the late renascence, which Kreymborg rightly dates from 1912. There are apparently two reasons for this. Since about 1880, the population of this country has more than doubled, and even in ratio to the present population, there can be no doubt that more verse is being written now than fifty years ago. Pending the collection of exact figures—which some scholar will probably give us very soon—we may guess that three, perhaps four times as much verse is written and published in the United States every year as in any year around 1880, when the New England movement reached its climax. We have more poets of talent; as Kreymborg remarks, our craftsmanship has improved enormously; we probably have five competent versifiers where there was one in 1850. But it is not certain that we have more great poets. If Mr. Kreymborg's intention had been to isolate the values of the past, instead of representing the poets by numbers, a procedure which throws the emphasis on the present, our era would surely not have received more space than the nineteenth century alone, to say nothing of the two preceding centuries taken with it. The second reason for the disproportionate attention given to our time is doubtless the author's complete contemporaneity. The vaguely evolutionary, progressive view of American poetry in this book puts the nineteenth-century giants in the role of forerunners, while we are the new brood of "national singers."

The chapters dealing with the past are first of all biographical, and then social in method. Beyond this, the writing is dithyrambic. There is ample evidence that the author has read practically every line of American poetry and that he has been moved by his reading; and yet industry and sensibility and enthusiasm will not take the place of insight, discrimination, intelligence. Written in bright, diffuse journalese, the chapters on the early poets are, in documentation, arrangement and evaluation of the subject, no better than half a dozen so-called standard histories of American literature. But it is not that Kreymborg lacks the material; he is not able to use it. Being an inveterate hero-worshipper, he prefers the vague rhetorical state-ment, not only to the meaning of the facts, but to a plain exposition of the facts, and he succeeds a little too often in making a legend of the commonplace. Because Miss Dickinson was a great poet, the stuffy and very ordinary life of a spinster is made the occasion for a painfully facetious piece of rhetoric. The myth of Whitman's disin-terested service in the Civil War hospitals is repeated, at Whitman's own evaluation of it; ten years of Whitman scholarship are ignored. Instead of taking Emerson's humanitarian activities as the key to a highly complex mind that never understood itself, Mr. Kreymborg is contented to view them, if he really views them at all, as evidence of a simple nobility of soul. The picture of Emerson is worth quoting in part: "Inside his serene domicile, at the heart of the clearest strength, this blue-eyed bard was in touch with all time and all life; and, in the marvelous fragments pieced together, whether in poetry or prose, he slowly created the song we know him by."

Mr. Kreymborg performs the difficult feat of making the lives of dead poets read like gossip. And the biographies of the living not only read like it, that is what they are. In the chapters on contemporary poets, there are eleven statements of fact that I know to be absolutely false, which could have been set down correctly if the author had taken the trouble to write the poets. In that center of vividly undifferentiated sensation which is Mr. Kreymborg's mind, there exist settled connections between life and poetry, fixed influences of one generation upon another, dogmatic if obscure assertions of the meaning of poetry, which must forever stir to envy and astonishment the mere plodder in immensely ambiguous and complicated fact. This work is one of those mischievously pious, utterly well meant documents which, like the writings of Poe's contemporary, Griswold, may have the effect of misleading public information and judgment for a quarter of a century. In the place of Griswold's malice (Mr. Kreymborg is uniformly benevolent), there is a gift for sentimental epithet that will seize the public fancy, and hold it for a long time.

For example. "At the height of her [Emily Dickinson's] intoxication, she leaned, not against a lamp-post, but against the sun of her adoration." "It is along the love line that Untermeyer has continued to develop." ". . . sonnets on the war full of disillusionment, though Ficke crossed the seas as a major." "In the course of seven swift years, she [Elinor Wylie] had finished four volumes of verse and four of prose. Then the mad flame sank." "Jeanne D'Orge, a student of the passions in relation to wedlock . . . " ". . . the yearning national question, where is our next major poet to come from . . . " "Over each group [of the younger poets] hangs an aura of metaphysics." Dorothy Parker is "haunted by modern metaphysics." And finally—

I bring the quotations to an arbitrary close—"One's hope for the art of the next Ishmael contains a plea for a less intellectual, a more human appeal."

Thus, the flood of emotionalism and self-expression which is, on the whole, the last fifteen years of American poetry, is "intellectualism" and "metaphysics." When Mr. Kreymborg is in doubt, he uses the word metaphysics. "In the presence of poetry," he writes, "definitions are unessential [sic] interlopers." (They are inessential when they are confused or fail to define; they are never interlopers.) It is remarkable, in view of this opinion, that the author should attempt so many definitions. Miss Millay's early, naughty spirit is the Restoration spirit and the spirit of Oscar Wilde; the three spirits are one, in a oneness that passeth understanding. The famous Euclid sonnet is an expression of "the poet's faith in the 'massive sandal set on stone'." Now, just how does this faith differ from the faith in Christ, or in Causality, or in Democracy? Or is it properly faith?

I come now to the "philosophy" of the work. One finds such phrases as the "synthesis of absolute poetry," poetry's "recent step ahead," progress, optimism and pessimism, acceptance of life, metaphysics and metaphysical poetry, roots in the soil, conservative and radical, belief in American democracy, and so on. I can find no very clear meaning in any of these phrases. However, there is a consistent if consistently inarticulate motive carrying the book to its final page. This motive, somewhat to the abuse of religion, must be called religious. It remains on the sentimental level. Our poetic history turns out to be a succession of prophets minor and major, like Forefather Bryant and Intoxicated Emerson, who with Walt, the maximus, and even the Weary Way-worn Wanderer, form an Old Testament prophesying a New Testament either already here or about to arrive. This state of mind, I believe, explains the barrier standing between Mr. Kreymborg and the poetry; his belief in Progress turns most of the poems into harbingers of other poems, other social conditons, other ages. There is, in this book, a certain uneasy expectancy of the true revelation which may be described as the obstetrical attitude of mind: our Shakespeare is due to be born, in the mechanical succession of Progress, whether he will be born or not. It would seem to me to be only common sense to suppose that we may some-time have a poet as great as Shakespeare, and equal common sense to see that it makes little difference whether we ever have him.

Yet Walt was the prophet and Mr. Kreymborg cannot repudiate the prophecy. He is not wholly at his ease, however, since he cannot understand why there is a *malaise* in the modern mind called "pes-simism," the prophet having foretold the perfect brotherhood, the perfect society and the "new brood." There is something discon-certingly wrong, from the Whitman viewpoint, with the new brood that has arrived, and our author does not like it; yet his "faith" in progress tells him that he ought to like it, though all the while he casts an apprehensive glance at the perfection and the liberties fore-told, now grown somewhat fatuous in their realization. The new Shakespeare may combine, as Mr. Kreymborg hopes, the love of Whitman and the hate of Jeffers, and he may combine many other things. One may hope that he will not mistake the size of his vision for its intelligence and quality.

From *The New Republic* (February 26, 1930)

Hart Crane

THE BRIDGE, a Poem, by Hart Crane. Limited edition, Paris: The Black Sun Press, 1930.

T HE VARIETY OF form and style that Mr. Crane successfully employs in this work testifies to his technical proficiency, and the richness of his poetic texture proves him to be endowed with gifts of the highest order. *The Bridge* is his second volume, and it more than fulfills the expectations aroused by the appearance of his first, *White Buildings,* in 1926. It is a collection of fifteen poems grouped in eight sections and tied together by a single theme. The subject of the poem derives from Brooklyn Bridge, which is at once fact, metaphor, and symbol; it quickly expands into a vision of an heroic American past and a divination of our spiritual future. Beyond this the theme is difficult to describe.

This difficulty appears at a glance to be the best proof of the poet's complete success: he everywhere transforms the subject into something rich and strange. The poem as a whole says vastly more than any literal paraphrase of it could possibly convey, if such a paraphrase could be written; for its logical meaning has an elusiveness that is singularly incompatible with the emotional intention, which is simple, and can be reduced to a phrase like "the grandeur of America" or "the magnificent future of America." Crane himself seems to have felt the discrepancy, for, following Coleridge, he has given us a marginal commentary on about half of the poem. This gloss, however, is obscure (though beautifully written), and it does not quite succeed with what I take its intention to be—to simplify the thread of the historical and symbolic continuity, by which the reader may proceed into the enormously complicated style.

The fifteen poems, taken as one poem, suffer from the lack of a coherent plot, whether symbolic or narrative: the coherence of the work consists in the personal quality of the writing—in mood, feeling, and tone. In the line by line texture, Mr. Crane has perfect mastery over the quality of his style; but it lacks an objective pattern of ideas elaborate enough to carry it through an epic or heroic work. The single symbolic image, round which the whole poem centers, is at one moment the actual Brooklyn Bridge; at another, it is any bridge or "connection"; at still another, it is a philosophical pun and becomes the basis of a series of analogies. In "Cape Hatteras," for example, the aeroplane and Walt Whitman are related "bridges" to some transcendental truth. The poet has not observed the distinction between a metaphor and a philosophical idea.

Because the idea is variously metaphor, symbol, and analogy, it tends to make the poem static. The poet takes it up, only to be forced to put it down again *when the poetic image of the moment is exhausted.* The idea does not, in short, fill the poet's mind; it is the starting point for a series of magnificent short flights, of beautiful inventions connected only in analogy—which explains the merely personal passages, which are obscure, and the lapses into sentimentality. The idea is not sufficiently objective and articulate in itself; it lags after the poet's vision; it appears and disappears; and in the intervals Crane improvises, often beautifully, as in the flight of the aeroplane, sometimes badly, as in the discourse on Whitman in the same poem.

In the great epic and philosophical works of our tradition, notably the *Divine Comedy,* the intellectual groundwork is not only simple philosophically; we not only know that the subject is personal salvation, just as we know that Mr. Crane's is the grandeur of America: we are given the complete articulation of the idea down to the slightest detail, and we are given it objectively apart from anything the poet is going to say about it. When the poet extends his perception, there is a further extension of the groundwork ready to meet it and discipline it, and to compel the invention of the poet to stick to the subject. It is a game of chess; neither side can move without consulting the other. Crane's difficulty is that of modern poets generally; they play the game with half of the men, the men of sensibility, and because they can make any move, the significance of all moves is obscure.

If we subtract from Crane's idea what he has to say about it, we have left only the static abstraction, "the grandeur of America," which is not only incapable of further elucidation on the logical plane, but actually obstructs it.

The theme of *The Bridge* is, in fact, an emotional over-simplification of a subject-matter that Crane did not, on the plane of narrative and fact, simplify at all. The poem is emotionally homogeneous and simple—it contains a single purpose; but because it is logically unclarified it is emotionally confused. America stands for a passage into new truths. Is this the meaning of American History? The poet has every right to answer yes, and this he has done. But just what in America or about America stands for this? Which American history? The historical plot of the poem, which is the groundwork on which the symbolic bridge stands, is arbitrary and broken, where the poet would have gained an overwhelming advantage by choosing a single period or episode, a concrete event with all its dramatic causes, and by following it up minutely, and being bound to it. In short, he would have gained an advantage could he have found a subject to stick to.

Does American culture afford such a subject? It probably does not. After the seventeenth century the sophisticated history of the scholars came into fashion; our popular, legendary chronicles come down only from the remoter European past. It is a sound impulse on Crane's part to look for an American myth, some simple version of our past that lies near the center of the American consciousness; an heroic tale with just enough symbolic morality to give his mind freedom and play. The soundness of his impulse is witnessed also by the kind of history in his poem: it is inaccurate, and it will not at all satisfy the sticklers for historical fact: it is the history of the motion picture, of the most naïve patriotism. This is sound; for it ignores the scientific ideal of truth-in-itself, and looks to a cultural truth which might win the spontaneous allegiance of the mass. It is on such simple integers of truth, not truth of fact but of religious necessity, that men unite. The American mind was formed on the eighteenth-century Enlightenment, which broke down the European truths and gave us a temper deeply hostile to the making of new religious truths of our own.

The impulse in *The Bridge* is religious, but the soundness of an impulse is no warrant that it will create a sound art form, which depends on too many factors beyond the control of the poet. The age is scientific and pseudo-scientific, and our philosophy is corrupt. And it is possibly this circumstance that has driven the religious attitude into a corner where it lacks the right instruments for its defense and growth, and where it is in a vast muddle about just what these instruments are. Perhaps this corruption of the intellect is responsible for Crane's unphilosophical belief that the poet, unaided and isolated from the people, can create a myth. If anthropology has destroyed the credibility of myths, it has shown us how they rise: their growth is mysterious from the people as a whole; and it is probable that no one man ever put myth into history. It is still a nice problem among higher critics, whether the authors of the Gospels were deliberate myth makers, or whether their minds were simply constructed that way; but the evidence favors the latter. Mr. Crane is a myth maker, and in an age favorable to myths he would have written a mythical poem in the act of writing an historical one.

For, American history being vast and disordered, and as various as American citizens (my own conception of it is radically different from Mr. Crane's), there was no settled version for the poet to draw upon and intensify. The episodes of *The Bridge* follow out of no inherent necessity in the theme, for they are arbitrary, and appear not organically but analogously. The form is static; each section is a new start, and but for the broken chronology the poem constantly begins over again.

It is difficult to agree with those critics who find the work a single poem and as such an artistic success. It is a collection of lyrics, the best of which are not surpassed by anything in American literature. The writing is most distinguished when Crane is least philosophical, *when he writes from sensation.* "The River" is a masterpiece of order and style; it alone is enough to place Crane in the first rank of American poets living or dead. Equally good but less ambitious are the "Proem: To Brooklyn Bridge," and "Harbor Dawn," and "The Dance" from the section called "Powhatan's Daughter."

These poems bear only the loosest sort of relation to the symbolic demands of the theme; they merely fit into the loose historical pattern or extend the slender structure of analogy running through the poem. They are primarily lyrical, and each has its complete form; it stands alone. The poem "Indiana," written presumably to complete the pattern of "Powhatan's Daughter," does not stand alone, and it is one of the most astonishing performances ever made by a poet of Crane's genius. "The Dance" gives us the American background for the coming white man, and "Indiana" carries the stream of history to the pioneer West. It is a nightmare of sentimentality and false writing: Crane is at his most philosophical in a theme in which he feels no poetic interest whatever.

The breakdown of the poem as an historical epic and the great distinction of the individual poems define, I believe, the range of Crane's poetry. It is lyrical. When he philosophizes explicitly in his verse, the doctrine is a sentimental muddle of Walt Whitman and the pseudo-primitivism of Sherwood Anderson and Dr. W. C. Williams, raised to a vague and transcendental reality. The impulse of the poem is, as I have said, religious, but in its lack of any religious structure it does not rise to a religious and tragic vision. Crane's vision is that of the naturalistic, romantic poet, and it vacillates between two poles. A buoyant optimism of the Whitman school and the direst Baudelairean pessimism exist side by side, unfused. The effect of that section of the poem intended as an Inferno, "The Tunnel," is largely nullified by the anti-climactic lapses into an infernal vision in the midst of panegyric. Crane's talent is romantic and mixed, and it does not survive the requirements of an extended objective pattern.

In this there is a similarity to the impulse of *Une Saison d'Enfer*; but there is a difference which is fundamental. Rimbaud achieved the mixed and disorganized surface of the poem by means of a process of deliberate dissociation. Crane begins with dissociation and tries to organize his pattern. In the case of Rimbaud there is a powerful intellectual drama resulting from his struggle against the intellectual order that he inherited; but Crane, at the end of the romantic movement, when the dissociation is all accomplished, struggles with the problem of finding an intellectual order. It is the romantic process reversed, and the next stage in the process is not romanticism at all.

Yet the very mixture of Crane's vision, when it stays on the lyrical plane, surcharges his verse with an inimitable richness of rhythm and style, and suffuses over it an untranslatable quality of immense poetic interest. In "The River" and "Harbor Dawn" he writes out of sensibility, and here his "philosophy" is an implicit pantheism which is harmless and without moral value, good or bad: it has no necessary consequence in any conceivable action. But, in the interpretation of American life implied in "The Bridge," there is the current apotheosis of the emotional will in its drive to mastery over mere quantities: truth is magnitude glimpsed on a remote plane. In his passive receptiveness—which is very different from a sound "wise passiveness" which Mr. Babbitt has misrepresented to the modern mind—and in his rejection of a rational and qualitative will, Crane follows the main stream of romanticism in the last hundred years. Starting with Poe, it came through Baudelaire and Rimbaud to American and English poets of the last generation. If this impulse is dying out, it is as fortunate for its reputation as it is remarkable, that it should be represented at the end by a poetry so rich, finely wrought, and powerful as Hart Crane's.

From *The Hound and Horn* (July–September, 1930)

T. S. Eliot

Ash Wednesday, by T. S. Eliot. The Fountain Press, 1930.

EVERY AGE, as it sees itself, is the peculiarly distracted one: its chroniclers notoriously make too much of the variety before their own eyes. We are now inclined to see the variety of the past as mere turbulence within a fixed unity, and our own surface standardization as the sign of a profound disunity of impulse. We have discovered that the chief ideas that men lived by from about the twelfth to the eighteenth century were absolute and unquestionable, and that the social turmoil of European history was simply shortsighted disagreement as to the best ways of making these deep assumptions socially good. The temper of literary criticism in the past appears to bear out this belief. Although writers were judged morally, no critic expected the poet to give him a morality. The standard of judgment was largely unconscious; a poem was a piece of free and disinterested enjoyment for minds mature enough—that is, convinced enough of a satisfactory destiny—not to demand of every scribbler a way of life. Dante invented no formula for society to run itself by; he only used a ready-made one. Turn to the American Humanists, and you will find that literature is the reflection of a secular order that must be controlled. But Mr. John Dos Passos has been far-sighted enough to detect the chief aim of modern criticism of nearly every school. This is: to give up the European and "belle-lettristic" dabbling with the arts, and all that that involves, and to study the American environment with a view to making a better adaptation to it.

To discuss the merits of such a critical outlook lies outside my argument. It would be equally pointless to attempt an appraisal of any of its more common guides to salvation, including the uncommon one of the Thirty-nine Articles, which have been subscribed to by Mr. T. S. Eliot, whose six poems published under the title *Ash Wednesday* are the occasion of this review. For it is my thesis that, in a discussion of Mr. Eliot's poetry, his doctrine has little to command interest in itself. Yet it appears that the poetry, notwithstanding the amount of space it gets in the critical journals, receives less discussion each year. The moral and religious attitude behind it has been related to the Thirty-nine Articles, to an intellectual position that Eliot has defended in prose. The poetry and the prose are taken together as evidence that the author has made a rather inefficient adaptation to the modern environment; or at least he doesn't say anything very helpful to the American critics in their struggles to adapt themselves. It is an astonishing fact that, in an atmosphere of "aesthetics," there is less discussion of poetry in a typical modern essay on that fine art than there is in Johnson's essay on Denham. Johnson's judgment is frankly moralistic, but he seldom capitulates to a moral sentiment because it flatters his own moral sense. He requires the qualities of generality, invention, and perspicuity. He hates Milton for a regicide, but his judgment of *Paradise Lost* is the most disinterested in English criticism. Mr. Eliot's critics are a little less able each year to see the poetry for Westminster Abbey; the wood is all trees.

I do not pretend to judge how far our social and philosophical needs justify this prejudice, which may be put somewhat summarily as follows: all forms of human action, economics, politics, even poetry, and certainly industry, are legitimate modes of salvation, but the more historical religious mode is illegitimate. It is sufficient here to point out that the man who expects to find salvation in the latest lyric or a well-managed factory will not only not find it there; he is not likely to find it anywhere else. If a young mind is incapable of moral philosophy, a mind without moral philosophy is incapable of understanding poetry. For poetry, of all the arts, demands a serenity of view and a settled temper of the mind, and most of all the power to detach one's own needs from the experience set forth in the poem. A moral sense so organized sets limits to the human enterprise, and is content to observe them. But if the reader lack this sense, the poem will be only a body of abstractions either useful or irrelevant to that body of abstractions already forming, but of uncertain direction, in the reader's mind. This reader will see the poem chiefly as biography, and he will proceed to deduce from it a history of the poet's case, to which he will attach himself if his own case resembles it; if it doesn't, he will reject it. Either way, the quality of the poem is ignored. But I will return to this in a moment.

The reasoning that is being brought to bear upon Mr. Eliot's recent verse is as follows: Anglo-Catholicism would not at all satisfy me; therefore, his poetry declines under its influence. Moreover, the poetry is not contemporaneous; it doesn't solve any labor problems; it is special, personal, and it can do us no good. Now the poetry *is* special and personal in quality, which is one of its merits, but what the critics are really saying is this—that his case-history is not special at all, that it is a general form of possible conduct that will not do for them. To accept the poetry seems to amount to accepting an invitation to join the Anglican Church. For the assumption is that the poetry and the religious position are identical. If this were so, why should not the excellence of the poetry induce them to join the Church, in the hope of writing as well, since the irrelevance of the Church to their own needs makes them reject the poetry? The answer is, of course, that both parts of this fallacy are common. There is an aesthetic Catholicism, and there is a Communist-economic rejection of art because it is involved with the tabooed mode of salvation.

The belief is that Mr. Eliot's poetry is a simple record of the relation of his personality to an environment, and it witnesses the powerful modern desire to judge an art scientifically, practically, industrially; according to how it works. The poetry is viewed as a pragmatic result, and it has no use. Now a different heredity-environment combination would give us, of mechanical necessity, a different result, a different quantity of power to do a different and perhaps better work. Doubtless this is true. But there is something disconcerting in this simple solution to the problem when it is looked at more closely. Two vastly different records or case-histories might give us, qualitatively speaking, very similar results: Baudelaire and Eliot have in common many qualities but *no history*. Their "results" have at least the common features of irony, humility, introspection, reverence—qualities fit only for contemplation and not for judgment according to their desirability in our own conduct.

It is in this, the qualitative sense, that Eliot's poetry has been, I believe, misunderstood. In this sense, the poetry is special, personal, of no use, and highly distinguished. But it is held to be a general formula, not distinct from the general formula that Eliot subscribed to when he went into the Church.

The form of the poems in *Ash Wednesday* is lyrical and solitary, and there is almost none of the elaborate natural description and allusion which gave *The Waste Land* a partly realistic and partly symbolic character. These six poems are a brief moment of religious experience in an age that believes religion to be a kind of defeatism and puts its hope for man in finding the right secular order. The mixed realism and symbolism of *The Waste Land* issued in irony. The direct and lyrical method of the new poems creates the simpler aesthetic quality of humility. The latter quality comes directly out of the former, and there is a nice continuity in Mr. Eliot's work.

In *The Waste Land* the prestige of our secular faith gave to the style its peculiar character. This faith was the hard, coherent medium through which the discredited forms of the historic religions emerged only to be stifled; the poem is at once their vindication and defeat. They are defeated in fact, as a politician may be defeated by the popular vote, but their vindication consists in the withering irony that their subordinate position casts upon the modern world.

The typical scene is the seduction of the typist by the clerk, in "The Fire Sermon." Perhaps Mr. J. W. Krutch has not discussed this scene, but a whole generation of critics have, and from a viewpoint that Mr. Krutch has recently made popular: the seduction betrays the romantic disillusion of the poet. The mechanical, brutal scene shows what love really is—that is to say, what it is scientifically, since science is Truth; it is only an act of practical necessity, for procreation. The telling of the story by the Greek seer, who is chosen from a past of illusion and ignorance, permits the scene to become a *satire on the foolish values of the past*. The values of the past were absurd and false; the scientific Truth is both true and bitter. This is the familiar romantic dilemma, and the critics have read it into the scene from their own romantic despair.

There is none in the scene itself. The critics, who being in the state of mind I have described are necessarily blind to an effect of irony, have mistaken the symbols of an ironic contrast for the terms of a philosophic dilemma. Mr. Eliot knows too much about classical irony to be overwhelmed by a doctrine in literary biology. For the seduction scene shows, not what man is, but what *for a moment* he thinks he is; in other words, the clerk stands for the secularization of the humane and qualitative values in the modern world. And the meaning of the contrast between Tiresias and the clerk is not disillusion, but irony. The scene is a masterpiece; perhaps the most profound vision that we have of modern man.

The importance of this scene as a key to the intention of *Ash Wednesday* lies in the moral identity of humility and irony and in an important difference between them artistically. Humility is subjective, a quality of the moral character, an habitual attitude. Irony is the particular and objective instance of humility—that is, it is an event or situation which induces humility in the mind of a spectator; it is that arrangement of experience, either premeditated by art or accidentally appearing in the affairs of men, which permits to the spectator an insight superior to that of the actor, and shows him that the practical formula, the special ambition, of the actor is bound to fail. Humility is thus the self-respect proceeding from a sense of the folly of men in their desire to dominate a natural force or situation. The seduction scene is the picture of the modern and dominating man. The cleverness and the pride of conquest of the "small house agent's clerk" are the badge of science, bumptious practicality, overweening secular faith. The very success of his conquest witnesses its aimless character; it succeeds as a wheel succeeds in turning; he can only do it over again.

His own failure to understand his position is irony, and the poet's insight into it is humility. This is essentially the poetic attitude, an attitude that Mr. Eliot has been approaching with increasing purity. It is not that his recent verse is better or more exciting than that of the period ending with *The Waste Land*. Actually it is less spectacular and less complex in subject-matter; for Eliot less frequently objectified his leading emotion, humility, into irony. His form is simple, expressive, homogeneous, and direct, and without the usual elements of violent contrast.

There is a single ironic passage in *Ash Wednesday*, and significantly enough it is the first stanza of the first poem. This passage presents objectively the poet *as he thinks himself for the moment to be*. It establishes that humility towards his own merit which sets the whole mood of the poems that follow. And the irony has been overlooked by the critics because they take the stanza as a literal exposition of the latest phase of the Eliot "case-history"—at a time when, in the words of Mr. Edmund Wilson, "his psychological plight seems most depressing." Thus, here is the pose of a Titan too young to be weary of strife, but weary of it nevertheless:

> Because I do not hope to turn again
> Because I do not hope
> Because I do not hope to turn
> Desiring this man's gift and that man's scope
> I no longer strive to strive towards such things
> (Why should the aged eagle stretch its wings?)
> Why should I mourn
> The vanished power of the usual reign?

If the six poems are taken together as the focus of a specific religious emotion, the opening stanza, instead of being a naïve personal "confession," becomes only a modest but highly effective technical performance. This stanza has two features that are necessary to the development of the unique imagery which distinguishes the religious emotion of *Ash Wednesday* from any other religious poetry of our time and which, in fact, probably makes it the only valid religious poetry we have. The first feature is the regular yet halting rhythm, the smooth uncertainty of movement which may either proceed to greater regularity or fall away into improvisation. The second feature is the imagery itself. It is trite; it echoes two familiar passages from English poetry. But the quality to be observed is this: it is secular imagery. It sets forth a special ironic emotion, but this emotion is not identified with any specific experience. The imagery is thus perfectly suited to the character of the rhythm. The stanza is a device for getting the poem under way, starting from a known and general emotion, in a monotonous rhythm, for a direction which to the reader is unknown. The ease, the absence of surprise, with which Mr. Eliot brings out the subject to be "discussed" is admi-

rable. After some further and ironic deprecation of his worldly powers, he goes on:

> And pray to God to have mercy upon us
> And pray that I may forget
> These matters that with myself I too much discuss
> Too much explain

We are being told, of course, that there is to be some kind of discourse on God, or a meditation; yet the emotion is still general. The
imagery is even flatter than before; it is imagery at all only in that
special context; for it is the diction of prose. And yet, subtly and
imperceptibly, the rhythm has changed; it is irregular and labored.
We are being prepared for a new and sudden effect, and it comes in
the first lines of the second poem:

> Lady, three white leopards sat under a juniper-tree
> In the cool of the day, having fed to satiety
> On my legs my heart my liver and that which had been
>   contained
> In the hollow round of my skull. And God said
> Shall these bones live? shall these
> Bones live?

From here on, in all the poems, there is constant and sudden change
of rhythm, and there is a corresponding alternation of two kinds of
imagery—the visual and tactile imagery common to all poetry and
without significance in itself for any kind of experience, and the
traditional religious symbols. The two orders are inextricably fused.

It is evident that Mr. Eliot has hit upon the only method now
available of using the conventional religious image in poetry. He has
reduced it to metaphor, to the plane of sensation. And corresponding to this process, there are images of his own invention which he
almost pushes over the boundary of sensation into abstractions, where
they have the appearance of conventional symbols. The passage I
have quoted above is an example of this: for the "Lady" may be a
nun, or even the Virgin, or again she may be a beautiful woman; but
she is presented, through the serious tone of the invocation, with
all the solemnity of a religious figure. The fifth poem exhibits the
reverse of the process; it begins with a series of plays on the Logos,

which is the most rarefied of all the Christian abstractions, and succeeds in creating an *illusion of sensation* by means of a broken and
distracted rhythm:

> If the lost word is lost, if the spent word is spent
> If the unheard, unspoken
> Word is unspoken, unheard;
> Still is the unspoken word, the word unheard,
> The word without a word, the Word within
> The world and for the world. . . .

From *The Hound and Horn* (January–March, 1931)

Roy Campbell

The Flaming Terrapin, by Roy Campbell. The Dial Press, 1924.
Adamastor, by Roy Campbell. The Dial Press, 1931.

IT IS JUST seven years since the appearance of *The Flaming Terrapin* introduced to the American public the interesting talent of Mr. Roy Campbell. The poem was reviewed extensively and, I believe, with something more than respect: I have revived it here to make the usual comparisons between the early and the more mature work of a poet. Moreover, Mr. Campbell's gifts offer more than the usual rewards of such comparisons. *Adamastor* is a distinguished book: it is not, I believe, receiving the attention it deserves. *The Flaming Terrapin* was merely interesting; it caused a sensation. It was facile, brilliant and hollow, owing to the failure of the poet to bring more than a pictorial rhetoric to bear upon a subject that required a little philosophical subtlety. It was, for these times, a very long poem. The new poems are short, well written and formally complete. They do not sprawl, as the early work sprawls on every page. The two volumes represent, so far as I have been able to find out, all of Mr. Campbell's published work except a long piece printed a few years ago in the French journal *Commerce*, which I have not seen.

The Flaming Terrapin is a single poem in six parts covering some eighty pages: I read it seven years ago, but I find it impossible to read it a second time to the end. The subject is a myth, possibly of African origin, which explains the world as controlled by a great terrapin, who is God, or the metaphysical ground of the universe. (The poet often makes it the latter, and thus *civilizes* his subject out of existence: this tends to make the work thin.) There are brilliant passages, and yet the grasp of the subject is almost entirely pictorial. A harder, more intellectual approach would have arranged the theme in its high and low points, and spaced out the emphases: there are, in Mr. Campbell's early style, no climaxes, but simply a constant opportunity for the highest flights of rhetoric. Now, far from being "modern," this defect is characteristic of the worst eighteenth-century poets; Mr. Campbell is more often nearer to Blackmore and Ambrose Phillips than to Rimbaud, to whose work for some reason *The Flaming Terrapin* has been compared. Phillips might have written these lines:

> The flying fishes in their silver mail
> Rose up like stars, and pattered down like hail,
> While the blunt whale, ponderous in his glee,
> Churned his broad flukes and siphoned up the sea,
> And through it as the creamy circles spread,
> Heaved the superb Olympus of his head.

This is Mr. Campbell's typical style:

> Sometimes the lord of nature in the air
> Spread forth his clouds and sable canvas, where
> His pencil, dipt in heavenly colors bright,
> Paints the fair rainbow, charming to the sight.

The lines are by Blackmore. Here is Ambrose Phillips:

> His nerves and muscles, like a wondrous lyre,
> Vibrated to that sound; and through his brain
> Proud thoughts came surging in a gorgeous train.

Mr. Campbell, not Phillips, wrote the lines, and against them there is the stock objection that the image is so elaborated beyond the inherent demands of the idea that it is ludicrous, and then very tiresome. There is unfortunately enough of this fault in the poem to hide its merits. Here is a beautiful passage spoiled by a nonsensical excess of image in the second line:

> When star by star, above the vaulted hill,
> The sky poured out its hoarded bins of gold,
> Night stooped upon the mountain tops, and still
> Those low concussions from the forest rolled. . . .

The third and fourth lines are among the most brilliant in contemporary verse, but we barely recover from the second line in time to appreciate them.

The poetry in *Adamastor* is much better. It is uneven, yet Mr. Campbell has found a way of relating his genius for imagery to a genuine center of feeling. The new poems are intelligently conceived, and the imagery is not decorative, but inherent. For the first time in Mr. Campbell's work, after the talk about it is over, there is a similarity to Rimbaud—not in any specific sense, but generally in the sense that his logic of imagery does not rest on a rational theme or argument, but rather on an emotion below (or above) reason which he succeeds in presenting with remarkable purity. Because the duration of this kind of emotion is necessarily brief, the best poems in the book range from fifteen to forty lines; beyond that length Mr. Campbell seldom knows where he is going, but within it he has written five or six poems that are among the best of their kind in this period. "Rounding the Cape," "The Zulu Girl," "African Moonrise" and notably "The Sisters" are unsurpassed by anything like them since the War—unless by Hart Crane's "Black Tambourine," which was written about ten years ago. Mr. Campbell's new poetry is extremely well written; it is versatile and charming; it is often witty, even when it is not distinguished. One hopes that he will write a great deal more poetry.

From *The New Republic* (March 18, 1931)

Babette Deutsch

Epistle to Prometheus, by Babette Deutsch. Jonathan Cape and Harrison Smith, 1931.

THE IDEA OF Prometheus does not appear to have called forth in Miss Deutsch either a depth of sensibility or a coherent scheme of ideas that might tend to clarify her imagery, which is rich, at times disconcertingly lush, occasionally irrelevant and, when it is irrelevant, in faulty taste. This is the worst that can, I believe, be said. There is also to be said a great deal of good.

The conception of the poem is extremely good. Being a modern, faithless, skeptical of myths and symbols, including the myth to which she addresses herself, Miss Deutsch refuses to approach the story of Prometheus directly; she uses an epistolary style and writes a commentary on it. To have taken a more conventional course and written an objective poem, in which the whole machinery of the Prometheus myth were set in motion would have implied in Miss Deutsch the act of accepting the myth as something more than a pretty story. This she was unable to do. Prometheus in this *Epistle* is as a symbol somewhat dim; the traditional outlines of the myth are sketched in just enough to give the poet a start in a series of loosely connected discourses on the meaning of the Fire-Bringer and some of the historical consequences of his theft.

This would seem to be ambitious; but I repeat that it is not. The intellectual honesty of a modern skeptic has whittled the myth down to the barest minimum. And the question that one must ask is this: If the poet did not intend to exhibit the myth in all its fullness and to tax her imagination with all its profound implications, why did she use the story at all? It might have been better if she had not. As it is, the development of her theme is a little like the predicament that General Hooker almost got his army in after the Battle of Chancellorsville—"like an ox half jumped over a fence, without a chance to gore one way or kick the other." Miss Deutsch's poem is never quite committed to the myth which is, in some sense, its subject; it is just enough involved in it to prevent her from developing her idea more fully apart from it.

This idea is, roughly, that the gift of Prometheus was not an unmitigated blessing. I think most reflective minds at present agree with this proposition; my objection is to the poet's exposition of it. The intellectual integrity that I have pointed out as guiding Miss Deutsch's approach to her theme should have, I believe, taken her a step farther; it might have left all myth behind and directed her to a purely subjective poem, which would have avoided that peculiar mixture and personal metaphor and objective symbol never quite yoked, even by violence. I think the truth is that Miss Deutsch, like most moderns, wished a large framework for her poem but did not care to put forth the imaginative effort to conceive it. By using a personal, subjective method of setting forth the simple proposition the Gift of Knowledge, of Foresight, of Applied Science, whatever you will, is evil, she could have avoided certain unnecessary lapses in style. For example, toward the end, occurs this passage:

> Yesterday was my birthday,
> without a guide (Trojan, Mantuan, Florentine—no matter),
> and look for none beside me at the end.
> I have come midway,
> walking with fallen arches through wilderness,
> midway through the dark wood,
> I have come.

Down to the two last lines the passage is pretty good allusion to Dante, but in the effort to lift it out of the commonplace she points up the ordinary phrase "footsore and weary" to "walking with fallen arches," which, somehow, does not fuse into the passage. It misses the intended symbolic value and sticks out as a piece of irrelevant fact, at which the reader murmurs it is none of his business.

This poem brings up a problem that can only be alluded to here: whether the failure of the modern mind to understand, to think itself into the great myths, is a failure of the religious attitude or a failure of the imagination; or whether the two failures are not the same. They probably are. Perhaps none of us could go farther than Miss Deutsch. It is not going very far. For, in place of the magnificent outlines and the full body of the myth, Miss Deutsch, trying to bring her work into form, breaks it up into little epistles, each preceded by a quotation setting forth the next subject—a confession that the framework cannot itself carry it clearly to the reader. To those who are interested in what it is now the fashion to call the "crisis in poetry," Miss Deutsch's *Epistle to Prometheus* will be an instructive text.

From the New York *Herald Tribune Books*
(April 26, 1931)

Edna St. Vincent Millay

Fatal Interview, by Edna St. Vincent Millay. Harper and Brothers, 1931.

MORE THAN any other living American poet, with the exception possibly of T. S. Eliot, Miss Millay has puzzled her critics. Contrary to the received opinion, her poetry is understood even less than Eliot's, in spite of its greater simplicity, its more conventional meters and its closer fulfilment of the popular notion of what the language of poetry should be. Of contemporary poets whose excellence is beyond much dispute, she is the most difficult to appraise. She is the most written about, but her critics are partisans: they like her too well or not enough. There is something like worship here, patronage or worse there; both views are unjust; and what is worse, they are misleading. Less interested readers of her verse are tired of violent opinion; the more skeptical, perhaps, are put off by her popularity in an age of famously indifferent taste.

This, too, is misleading. Apart from her merit as a poet, Miss Millay is, not at all to her discredit, the spokesman of a generation. It does not behoove us to enquire how she came to express the feelings of the literary generation that seized the popular imagination from about 1917 to 1925. It is a fact that she did, and in such a way as to remain as its most typical poet. Her talent, with its diverting mixture of solemnity and levity, won the enthusiasm of a time bewildered intellectually and moving unsteadily towards an emotional attitude of its own. It was the age of *The Seven Arts*, of the old *Masses*, of the Provincetown Theatre, of the figure and disciples of Randolph Bourne. It has been called the age of experiment and liberation; there is still experiment, but no one is liberated; and that age is now dead.

119

Miss Millay helped to form that generation, and was formed by it. But she has survived her own time. Her statement about those times, in *A Few Figs from Thistles* and *Second April*, was not, taken philosophically, very profound; morally, it has been said, it did perceptible damage to our young American womanhood, whose virgin impatience competed noisily with the Armistice and the industrial boom. There were suicides after *Werther* and seductions after *Don Juan*. Neither Byron nor Miss Millay is of the first order of poets. They are distinguished examples of the second order, without which literature could not bear the weight of Dante and Shakespeare, and without which poetry would dry up of insensibility.

Being this kind of poet, Miss Millay was not prepared to give to her generation a philosophy in comprehensive terms; her poetry does not define the break with the nineteenth century. This task was left to the school of Eliot, and it was predictable that this school should be—except by young men who had the experience to share Eliot's problem—ignored and misunderstood. Eliot penetrated to the fundamental structure of the nineteenth-century mind and showed its breakdown. Miss Millay assumed no such profound alteration of the intelligence because, I suppose, not being an intellect but a sensibility, she was not aware of it. She foreshadowed an age without bringing it to terms. Taking the vocabulary of nineteenth-century poetry as pure as you will find it in Christina Rossetti, and drawing upon the stock of conventional symbolism accumulated from Drayton to Patmore, she has created, out of shopworn materials, a distinguished personal idiom: she has been able to use the language of the preceding generation to convey an emotion peculiar to her own.

The generation of decadence—Moody, Woodberry and Louise Imogene Guiney—had more than Miss Millay has; but she has all that they had which was not dead. By making their language personal she has brought it back to life. This is her distinction. It is also her limitation. As a limitation it is not peculiar to her, her age or any age, but common to all; it is the quality that defines Collins and Gray, and, in the next century, poets like the Rossettis and Tennyson. Poets of this second order lack the power of creation in the proper sense in which something like a complete world is achieved, either in the vast, systematic vision of Milton, or in the allusive power of Webster and Shakespeare where, backed only by a piece of common action, an entire world is set up in a line or even in a single phrase. In these poets the imaginative focus is less on the personal emotion than on its substructure, an order of intellectual life, and thus their very symbolism acquires not only a heightened significance but an independent existence of its own. Not so with Miss Millay; we feel that she never penetrates to the depth of her symbols, but uses them chiefly as a frame of reference, an adornment to the tale. It has been frequently and quite justly remarked that Miss Millay uses her classical symbols perhaps better than any other living poet; we should add, I believe, that she uses them conventionally better. She takes them literally, subtracting from them always only what serves her metaphor; whereas even a modern like Yeats is capable, in his sonnet "Leda," of that violent addition to the content of the symbol as he finds it which is the mark of great poetry.

Miss Millay's success with stock symbolism is precariously won. I have said that she is not an intellect but a sensibility: if she were capable of a profound analysis of her imagery she might not use it: such an analysis might disaffect her with the style that she so easily assumed, without necessarily leading her, as Yeats was led in mid-career, to create a new style of her own. The beautiful final sonnet of the sequence is a perfect specimen of her talent, and it is probably the finest poem she has written:

> Oh, sleep forever in the Latmian cave,
> Mortal Endymion, darling of the moon!
> Her silver garments by the senseless wave
> Shouldered and dropped and on the shingle strewn,
> Her fluttering hand against her forehead pressed,
> Her scattered looks that trouble all the sky,
> Her rapid footsteps running down the west—
> Of all her altered state, oblivious lie!
> Whom earthen you, by deathless lips adored,
> Wild-eyed and stammering to the grasses thrust,
> And deep into her crystal body poured
> The hot and sorrowful sweetness of the dust:
> Whereof she wanders mad, being all unfit
> For mortal love, that might not die of it.

We have only to compare this, magnificent as it is, with Mr. Yeats's "Leda" to see the difference between the two kinds of symbol that I have described. The difference is first of all one of concentration and intensity; and finally a difference between an accurate picture of an emotion and an act of the imagination:

> A sudden blow: the great wings beating still
> Above the staggering girl, her thighs caressed
> By the dark webs, her nape caught in his bill,
> He holds her helpless breast upon his breast.
>
> How can those terrified vague fingers push
> The feathered glory from her loosening thighs?
> And how can body, laid in that white rush
> But feel the strange heart beating where it lies?
> A shudder in the loins engenders there
> The broken wall, the burning roof and tower
> And Agamemnon dead.
>   Being so caught up,
> So mastered by the brute blood of the air,
> Did she put on his knowledge with his power
> Before the indifferent beak could let her drop?

In an age which, in Mr. Pound's phrase, has "demanded an image"; an age which has searched for a new construction of the mind, and has, in effect, asked every poet for a chart of salvation, it has been forgotten that one of the most valuable kinds of poetry may be deficient in imagination, and yet be valuable for the manner in which it meets its own defect. Miss Millay not only has given the personality of her age, but has preserved it in the purest traditional style. There are those who will have no minor poets; these Miss Millay does not move. The others, her not too enthusiastic but perhaps misguided partisans, have seen too much of their own personalities in her verse to care whether it is great poetry or not; so they call it great.

It is doubtful if all of Miss Millay's previous work put together is worth the thin volume of those fifty-two sonnets. At no previous time has she given us so sustained a performance. Half of the sonnets, perhaps all but about fifteen, lack distinction of emotional quality. None is deficient in an almost final technique. From first to last every sonnet has its special rhythm and sharply defined imagery; they move like a smooth machine, but not machine-like, under the hand of a masterly technician. The best sonnets would adorn any of the great English sequences. There is some interesting analysis to be made of Miss Millay's skillful use of the Shakespearean form, whose difficult final couplet she has mastered, and perhaps is alone in having mastered since Shakespeare.

The serious, austere tone of her later work must not deceive us: she is the poet of ten years ago. She has been from the beginning the one poet of our time who has successfully stood athwart two ages; she has put the personality of her age into the intellect and style of the preceding one, without altering either. Of her it may be said, as of the late Elinor Wylie, that properly speaking she has no style, but has subtly transformed to her use the indefinable average of poetic English. We have seen the limitations of this order of talent. When the personal impulse lags in a mind that cannot create a symbol and invent a style, we get the pastiche of *The Buck in the Snow*: the defects of such a talent are defects of taste, while the defects of Blake are blunders. Let us say no more of it. Miss Millay is one of our most distinguished poets, and one that we should do well to misunderstand as little as possible.

From *The New Republic* (May 6, 1931)

Ezra Pound

A Draft of XXX Cantos, by Ezra Pound. Paris: The Hours Press. Edition of 212 copies, 1930.

I

> and as for text we have taken it
> from that of Messire Laurentius
> and from a codex once of the Lords Malatesta . . .

ONE IS NOT certain who Messire Laurentius was; one is not very certain that it makes no difference. Yet one takes comfort in the vast range of Mr. Pound's obscure learning, which no one man could be expected to know much about. In this great work one is continually uncertain, as to space, time, history. The codex of the Lords Malatesta would be less disconcerting than Laurentius—if we were sure it existed—for more than half of the thirty cantos contain long paraphrases or garbled quotations from the correspondence, public and private, of the Renaissance Italians, chiefly Florentine and Venetian. About a third of the lines are versified documents. Another third are classical allusions, esoteric quotations from the ancients, fragments of the Greek poets with bits of the Romans thrown in; all magnificently written into Mr. Pound's own text. The rest is contemporary—anecdotes, satirical pictures of vulgar Americans, obscene stories, evenings in low Mediterranean dives, and gossip about amazing rogues behind the scenes of European power. The three kinds of material in the cantos are antiquity, the Renaissance, and the modern world. They are combined on no principle that seems in the least consistent to a first glance. They appear to be mixed in an incoherent jumble, or to stand up in puzzling contrasts.

This is the poetry which, in early and incomplete editions, has had more influence on us than any other of our time; it has had an immense underground reputation. And deservedly. For even the early reader of Mr. Pound could not fail to detect the presence of a new poetic form in the individual cantos; though the full value and intention of this form appears for the first time in the complete work. It is not that there is any explicit feature of the whole design that is not contained in each canto; it is simply that Mr. Pound must be read in bulk; it is only then that the great variety of his style and the apparent incoherence turn into order and form. There is no other poetry like the *Cantos* in English. And there is none quite so simple in form. The form is, in fact, so simple that almost no one has guessed it, and I suppose it will continue to puzzle, perhaps to enrage, our more academic critics for a generation to come. But this form by virtue of its simplicity remains inviolable to critical terms: even now it cannot be technically described.

I begin to talk like Mr. Pound, or rather like the way in which most readers think Mr. Pound writes. The secret of his form is this: conversation. The cantos are talk, talk, talk; not by any one in particular to any one else in particular; they are just rambling talk. At least each canto is a cunningly devised imitation of a polite conversation, in which no one presses any subject very far. The length of breath, the span of conversational energy, is the length of the canto. The conversationalist pauses; there is just enough left hanging in the air to give him a new start; so that the transitions between the cantos are natural and easy.

Each canto has the broken flow and the somewhat elusive climax of a good monologue: because there is no single speaker, it is a many-voiced monologue. That is the method of the poems—though there is another quality of the form that I must postpone for a moment—and *that is what the poems are about*.

There are, as I have said, three subjects of conversation—ancient times, Renaissance Italy, and the present—but these are not what the cantos are about. They are not about Italy, not about Greece, nor are they about us. They are not about anything. But they are distinguished poetry. Mr. Pound himself tells us:

> And they want to know what we talked about?
>   *"de litteris et de armis, praestantibus que ingeniis,*

Both of ancient times and our own; books, arms,
And men of unusual genius
Both of ancient times and our own, in short the usual subjects
Of conversation between intelligent men."

II

There is nothing in the cantos more difficult than that. There is
nothing inherently obscure; nothing too profound for any reader who
has enough information to get to the background of all the allusions
in a learned conversation. But there is something that no reader,
short of some years of hard textual study, will understand. This is
the very heart of the cantos, the secret of Mr. Pound's poetic character, which will only gradually emerge from a detailed analysis of
every passage. And this is no more than our friends are constantly
demanding of us; we hear them talk, and we return to hear them
talk, and we return to hear them talk again, but we never know
what they talk about; we return for that mysterious quality of charm
that has no rational meaning that we can define. It is only after a
long time that the order, the direction, the rhythm of the talker's
mind, the logic of his character as distinguished from anything logical he may say—it is a long time before this begins to take on form
for us. So with Mr. Pound's cantos. It is doubtless easier for us (who
are trained in the more historic brands of poetry) when the poems
are about God, Freedom, and Immortality, but there is no reason
why poetry should be so perplexingly simple as Mr. Pound's, and be
about nothing at all.

The ostensible subjects of the cantos—ancient, middle, and modern times—are only the materials round which Mr. Pound's mind
plays constantly; they are the screen upon which he throws a beautiful, flowing quality of poetic thought. Now in conversation the
memorable quality is a sheer accident of character, and is not de-
signed; but in the cantos the effect is deliberate, and from the first
canto to the thirtieth the set tone is maintained without a single
lapse.

It is this tone, it is this quality quite simply, which is the meaning
of the cantos, and although, as I have said, it is simple and direct, it
is just as hard to pin down, it is as hidden in its shifting details, as

a running, ever-changing conversation. It cannot be taken out of the text; and yet the special way that Mr. Pound has of weaving his three materials together, of emphasizing them, of comparing and contrasting them, gives us a clue to the leading intention of the poems. I come to that quality of the form which I postponed.

The easiest interpretation of all poetry is the symbolic method: there are few poems that cannot be paraphrased into a kind of symbolism, which is usually false, being by no means the chief intention of the poet. It is very probable, therefore, that I am about to falsify the true simplicity of the cantos into a simplicity that is merely convenient and spurious. The reader must bear this in mind, and view the slender symbolism that I am going to read into the cantos as a critical shorthand, useful perhaps, but which when used must be dropped.

One of the finest cantos is properly the first. It describes a voyage:

> And then went down to the ship,
> Set keel to breakers, forth on the godly sea, and
> We set up mast and sail on that swart ship,
> Bore sheep aboard her, and our bodies also
> Heavy with weeping, and winds from sternward
> Bore us out onward with bellying canvas,
> Circe's this craft, the trim-coifed goddess.

They land, having come "to the place aforesaid by Circe"—whatever place it may be—and Tiresias appears, who says:

> "Odysseus
> Shalt return through spiteful Neptune, over dark seas,
> Lose all companions." And then Anticlea came.
> Lie quiet Divus. I mean, that is, Andreas Divus,
> In officina Wecheli, 1538, out of Homer.
> And he sailed, by Sirens and thence outward and away
> And unto Circe.

Mr. Pound's world is the scene of a great Odyssey, and everywhere he lands it is the shore of Circe, where men "lose all companions" and are turned into swine. It would not do at all to push this hint too far, but I will risk one further point: Mr. Pound is a typically modern, rootless, and internationalized intelligence. In the place of the traditional supernaturalism of the older and local cultures, he has a cosmopolitan curiosity which seeks out marvels, which are all equally marvelous, whether it be a Greek myth or the antics in Europe of a lady from Kansas. He has the bright, cosmopolitan savoir faire which refuses to be "taken in": he will not believe, being a traditionalist at bottom, that the "perverts, who have set money-lust before the pleasures of the senses," are better than swine. And ironically, being modern and a hater of modernity, he sees all history as deformed by the trim-coifed goddess.

The cantos are a book of marvels—marvels that he has read about, or heard of, or seen; there are Greek myths, tales of Italian feuds, meetings with strange people, rumors of intrigues of state, memories of remarkable dead friends like T. E. Hulme, comments on philosophical problems, harangues on abuses of the age; the "usual subjects of conversation between intelligent men."

It is all fragmentary. Now nearly every canto begins with a bit of heroic antiquity, some myth, or classical quotation, or a lovely piece of lyrical description in a grand style. It invariably breaks down. It trails off into a piece of contemporary satire, or a flat narrative of the rascality of some Italian prince. This is the special quality of Mr. Pound's form, the essence of his talk, the direction of these magnificent conversations.

For not once does Mr. Pound give himself up to any single story or myth. The thin symbolism from the Circe myth is hardly more than a leading tone, an unconscious prejudice about men which he is not willing to indicate beyond the barest outline. He cannot believe in any of them, not even in his own power of imagining them out to a conclusion. None of his myths is compelling enough to draw out his total intellectual resources; none goes far enough to become a belief or even a momentary faith. They remain marvels to be looked at, but they are meaningless, the wrecks of civilization. His powerful juxtapositions of the ancient, the Renaissance, and the modern worlds reduce all three elements to an unhistorical miscellany, timeless and without origin, and no longer a force in the lives of men.

III

And that is the peculiarly modern quality of Mr. Pound. There is a certain likeness in this to another book of marvels, those stories of late antiquity known to us as *The Golden Ass*. The cantos are a sort of *Golden Ass*. There is a likeness, but there is no parallel beyond the mere historical one: both books are the production of worlds without convictions and given over to a hard secular program. Here the similarity ends. For Mr. Pound is a powerful reactionary, a faithful mind devoted to those ages when the myths were not merely pretty, but true. And there is a cloud of melancholy irony hanging over the cantos. He is persuaded that the myths are only beautiful, and he drops them after a glimpse, but he is not reconciled to this aestheticism: he ironically puts the myths against the ugly specimens of modern life that have defeated them. But neither are the specimens of modernity worthy of the dignity of belief:

> She held that a sonnet was a sonnet
> And ought never to be destroyed
> And had taken a number of courses
> And continued with hope of degrees and
> Ended in a Baptist learnery
> > Somewhere near the Rio Grande.

I am not certain that Mr. Pound will agree with me that he is a traditionalist; nor am I convinced that Mr. Pound, for his part, is certain of anything under heaven but his genius for poetry. He is probably one of two or three living Americans who will be remembered as poets of the first order. Yet there is no reason to infer from that that Mr. Pound, outside his craft, or outside his conversation, knows in the least what he is doing or saying. He is and always has been in a muddle of revolution; and for some appalling reason he identifies his crusade with liberty—liberty of speech, liberty of press, liberty of conduct—in short, liberty. I do not mean to say that either Mr. Pound or his critic knows what liberty is. Nevertheless, Mr. Pound identifies it with civilization and intelligence, of the modern and scientific variety. And yet the ancient cultures, which he so much admires, were, from any modern viewpoint, hatched in barbarism and superstition. One is entitled to the suspicion that Mr. Pound prefers barbarism, and that by taking up the role of revolution against it he has bitten off his nose to spite his face. He is the confirmed enemy of provincialism, never suspecting that his favorite, Lorenzo the Magnificent, for example, was provincial to the roots of his hair.

This muddle runs through the cantos, and it makes the irony that I have spoken of to a certain extent unconscious. For as the apostle of humane culture, he constantly discredits it by crying up a rationalistic enlightenment. It would appear from this that his philosophical tact is somewhat feminine, and that, as intelligence, it does not exist. His poetic intelligence is of the finest: and if he doesn't know what liberty is, he understands poetry, and how to write it. This is enough for one man to know. And the thirty cantos are enough to occupy a loving and ceaseless study—say a canto a year for thirty years, all thirty to be read every few weeks just for the tone.

From *The Nation* (June 10, 1931)

Conrad Aiken

The Melody of Chaos, by Houston Peterson. Longmans, Green and Company, 1931.

IT IS COMFORTING to know that Mr. Peterson's exhaustive analysis of the work of Conrad Aiken was begun while the poet was still a legend to that public to which he has been recently introduced by a Pulitzer prize. This study of Aiken was planned and indeed partly written before the *Selected Poems* appeared in the autumn of 1929. To Mr. Peterson, therefore, must go the credit of being the first critic to see the poet's work as a whole and to discover in it a philosophical design, an "intellectual program," that has been overlooked by all previous critics whatever. Among these the present reviewer testifies to his own presence. Mr. Aiken is one of the most prolific poets of his time: during the twenty years of his career the critics have been criminally inattentive. But suddenly, alone of his generation, Mr. Aiken is the subject of a large critical volume.

Mr. Peterson is well qualified for the task as he conceives it. He has a minute and sympathetic knowledge of Aiken's entire work; he has besides a respectable philosophical learning, from which he sketches the background of the poet's ideas; and he knows the literature of romanticism. All this he brings to bear upon his subject. His method is admirable. In the first chapter, "Mania Psychologica," he describes the contemporary interest in the mooted existence, the nature, the function and the limits of consciousness—as distinguished from the nineteenth-century preoccupation with astronomy and biology. This is familiar ground. But Mr. Peterson's argument is always directed to his task, which is to show that Aiken has examined consistently, in one long poem after another, all the implications of the modern belief in a discrete and pluralistic soul. He is, therefore, says Mr. Peterson, the philosophical poet of his generation.

Each long poem receives a chapter. Written in 1915, the first of these is *The Charnel Rose*, a study in nympholepsy, the extreme form of romantic idealism; it foreshadows the poet's later and fully developed interest in specific theories of psychology. *The Jig of Forslin*, a study in "vicarious experience," exhibits this interest full-fledged; it is the exploration of the mind of a man in a great modern city, who is cut off from direct experience—a living instance of the drift of psychological theory toward the idea of a mind without individuality or personal identity. *The House of Dust* carries on the experiment, and anticipates Joyce, in part, as well as the *unanimisme* of Romains, Waldo Frank and Virginia Woolf. The next poem goes further: *Senlin* is a piece of speculation on the existence of personal identity itself. And it is followed by a somewhat more dramatic poem, *The Pilgrimage of Festus*, which delves into the miscellaneous compulsions of the ego that leave the poet skeptical of the reality of the self in the medieval sense. *Punch: The Immortal Liar* is a buffoon driven by a psychological mechanism—a buffoon because he is so driven. While these poems were being written, Mr. Aiken was developing the theme of the *danse macabre*, in what are probably his two best and most powerful poems—the early "Tetelestai" and the allegory "John Deth," the most recent of the longer works.

Not only for his subject but for contemporary poetry, Mr. Peterson does a great service in showing that Aiken was the pioneer of many methods usually accredited to other poets. *The Jig of Forslin* is perhaps the first poem in English whose structure is at once "symphonic" and philosophical in the manner in which *The Waste Land* is a mixture of meditation and musical effect. Fletcher's symphonies, of course, anticipate Aiken's, but theirs is a method apart. Aiken's originality lies in his brilliant adaptation of Fletcher's method to the moral implications of psychological theory. The interwoven melodies and symbols, the contrapuntal repetition of theme, become the obvious vehicle of the subrational lives of his characters. Mr. Peterson takes a particular and just pleasure in censuring the early, short-sighted opinions of Mr. Aiken's early poems. Aldous Huxley, for example, reviewed *The House of Dust* in *The Nation and Athenaeum* in 1920, but ignored the prefatory remarks on the poetical possibilities of musical form: several years later, in *Point Counter Point*, as the title implies, Huxley described his own intention: "The musicalization of fiction. Not in the symbolist way . . . but on a large scale, in the construction." As Mr. Peterson says, this was precisely Aiken's intention in *The House of Dust*. In the same review, however, Huxley writes a criticism of Aiken not so easily refuted.

He says: ". . . he will have to find some new intellectual formula into which to concentrate the shapelessness of his vague emotions." Peterson replies: ". . . the outstanding merit of Aiken's poetry is its intellectual formula, which no other author has elaborated so rigorously or so effectively." Whether or not Huxley is at fault and I think he is for imprecision, Mr. Peterson apparently misses the drift of his criticism, and thus fails to get to the heart of the problem that Aiken's long poems try to solve.

Admittedly Mr. Aiken has his formulas, and admittedly he gets them from the psychologists. Why then should we not go directly to them rather than to Mr. Aiken? Taken over as literally as Mr. Aiken takes them (with that romantic naïveté which eagerly seizes upon the terrible truth) and dissipated by metaphor, they collapse in the "shapelessness" that Huxley remarked. The poems are beautifully written, but they have no direction. A psychological theory of disunity makes this inevitable; nor are we consoled by reflecting that back of the poetry there may be psychological truth—a truth more coherently expressed, however, by the psychologists. Psychology cannot give to art a compelling and unifying symbol of its picture of a multiple soul. It is not that Mr. Aiken lacks intellectual forumulas, but rather that he has too many that are not sharply differentiated and brought to heel by the imagination. The people in *Troilus and Cressida* suffer the moral disorganization that is supposed to follow after modern psychology; but Shakespeare's method is not in the least disorganized. Moreover, the imitation of disorder that Eliot achieves in *The Waste Land* is very different from Mr. Aiken's aimlessness—an effect produced by a constant elaboration of metaphor unrelieved by any of those illuminating statements with which Webster will suddenly draw a whole play together. Mr. Aiken's intellectual formulas (with an exception to be noticed) do not permit him to make any artistically unifying statements about his disorder. This is one of the faults of the nineteenth-century romanticism from which he derives.

But his case is different from that of the English romantics, who could still use the ready-made forms of medievalism and the classical world. His substitute for external form becomes a method of exposition based on musical analogy, which is very different from an actual musical composition. The absolute abstraction of subject matter necessary to musical form constantly wars with the emotional, imagistic and rational content, whose tendency is always toward logical form. Moreover, the logical and the musical forms require different spans of attention; the musical rhythm twists or thins out the subject matter; and the proper emphases of the subject matter violate the right periods and elaborations of musical form.

The single important work of Mr. Aiken's that avoids the perils of psychological theory and musical form is the beautiful allegory of the dance of death, "John Deth," which I feel that Mr. Peterson with too little zeal confesses a masterpiece. Here for the first time Mr. Aiken has found a simple, comprehensive idea, whose philosophical meaning is at all points identical with a rich symbolism and interchangeable with it; fully rounded and self-contained; having within itself, in the natural progression from birth to death, a formal limitation that gives direction to the hitherto wandering structure of the symphonic poems. Here is an intellectual formula which is more than that. Not only this, but Mr. Aiken's imagery is more concentrated and his verse stronger. We must not be alarmed when Mr. Peterson tells us that the germ of the poem is in Freud's *Beyond the Pleasure Principle,* for the conception of life as the medium in which the organism must wear itself out toward its goal in death is as old as Western culture.

Perhaps Mr. Peterson—in spite of a certain impressionism of style which permits him to write phrases like "blank despair" and the "cruel austerity" of Hemingway—perhaps Mr. Peterson is a somewhat too intellectual man, and not in the very best sense. It is doubtful if he distinguishes a difference between the intellectual formulas of *Senlin* and "John Deth." He is inclined to rest his case for Mr. Aiken on his discovery that the poetry has a wide range of modern ideas; having made this discovery, he seems to feel that it is necessarily a discovery of great poetry. Poetry and a large range of ideas often go together; but neither proves the existence of the other. Whether Mr. Aiken is a great poet is a question for future criticism. Mr. Peterson is expository and interpretative, but not, with respect to the poetic quality, critical. And this is the reason why he is unkind to Mr. Aiken's contemporaries, notably T. S. Eliot, whose *Waste Land*, in its "symphonic" character, *The Jig of Forslin* anticipated; he feels that Aiken's priority makes him superior. Eliot's poem has been widely praised, and Aiken's comparatively neglected, because Eliot's is the better poem.

From *The New Republic* (July 22, 1931)

Aldous Huxley

The Cicadas and Other Poems, by Aldous Huxley. Doubleday, Doran & Co., 1931.

MR. HUXLEY has never written badly, and his verse is quite as well-written as his prose; but it is not so good. His mind, I believe, is chiefly a prose mind: it requires a good deal of purely statistical circumstance (which, as such, poetry abhors) to make its most telling effects. His verse is full of interesting, accurately observed images, yet they have a fatal deadness about them, as if they had not sprung out of an idea or out of a total grasp of his subject, but had been noted down:

> All day the wheels turn;
> All day the roaring of the wheels, the rasping,
> Weave their imprisoning lattices of noise.

This is the germ of a good prose paragraph: the image of the lattices has no roots in the central idea, it is merely an item in a list. To make a momentary distinction, one may say that Mr. Huxley has observation but little perception. The verse is competently turned out; it is overloaded with too much miscellaneous imagery that cancels itself; it is almost as if Mr. Huxley heaped up his metaphors in order to give the hue of poetry to the philosophical point that, like Arnold, he cannot keep from arguing. "Picture by Goya," however, is in a kind of Rimbaudian symbolist style, a pyrotechnical mixture of the modes of feeling; it is the modern "exacerbated sensibility" of a man who is still fascinated by the doubt-faith dilemma of the seventies. There is a good deal of Arnold in Huxley, who is a better versifier on the whole, but never up to Arnold's best.

136

One hesitates to say that Mr. Huxley is not a poet; he has about three times as much craftsmanship as many born poets (Arnold, for one). His translation of "Femmes Damnées" is the best ever made; I regret only the failure to reproduce more of the exact shade of emphasis in the famous transitional passage beginning *"Descendez, descendez, lamentables victimes,"* a verse that Huxley somewhat lamely renders, "Hence, lamentable victims, get you hence." Here Mr. Huxley's technical skill is sustained by an impulse more powerful than his own; the poem is the best in the book.

There are fifteen sonnets on the decay of European life—a theme that Huxley sees rather from the viewpoint of "Dover Beach"—to which he brings a sensitive, civilized mind looking ironically upon the ruins; but the poetic interest of the sonnets is not great. One feels that the new poems, for all their greater finish, their smoother efficiency of versification, lack the virtues of the far cruder "Philosopher's Songs" in *Leda*; these early poems, in spite of the facile derivation from Laforgue, had considerable vigor and promised the growth of an interesting talent that wisely or not has created Mr. Huxley's more serious prose. These lines are the best Huxley; to enjoy them one must get used to a purely rhetorical quality of image:

> Time passes, and the watery moonrise peers
> Between the tree-trunks. But no outer light
> Tempers the chances of our groping years,
> No moon beyond our labyrinthine night.
>
> Clueless we go; but I have heard thy voice,
> Divine Unreason, harping in the leaves,
> And grieve no more; for wisdom never grieves,
> And thou hast taught me wisdom; I rejoice.

From *Poetry* (February, 1932)

E. E. Cummings

Viva (seventy new poems), by E. E. Cummings. Horace Liveright, Inc., 1931.

THE OCCASION of this review is unfortunately a single book by Mr. Cummings, and the opportunity for generalization about his work as a whole is slight. But it is an opportunity that must be seized, if the reviewer intends to say anything at all: the quality of *Viva*, being quite uniform with that of its predecessors, imposes upon the reviewer no obligation to announce to the public important changes, in Mr. Cummings' work, of style, composition, or point of view. This fact alone is, of course, of no significance, but it brings to the reviewer a grateful feeling of relief; it permits him to write with a full sense of the merit of the three previous books of verse by this poet, a sense that corrects, as it should, a feeling of disappointment in the quality of *Viva*.

It is not that the quality has "fallen off." Cummings' faults are well-known, I believe, if not generally defined, and they are still essentially the faults of *Tulips and Chimneys*. In that volume it was not easy to distinguish his own quality, and thus his limitations, from the influence of other poets, Keats and Swinburne; but this influence has disappeared. The special quality of his talent stands forth without the misleading features of an unformed style. He has refined his talent, perhaps not to the point of which it is ideally capable, but at least to the point at which he is able to convey the particular kind of meaning that very properly obsesses any poet in contact with his medium. From first to last his work has shown the growth of a uniform quality, and a progressive tendency to define that quality with a certain degree of purity.

138

His uniformity is not uniformity of style. The point could be labored, but I think it is sufficient to refer the reader of Cummings to the three distinct styles of poems *XVIII*, *LI*, and *LVII* in *Viva*. He has a great many styles, and having these he has none at all—a defect concealed by his famous mechanism of distorted word and line. For a style is that indestructible quality of a piece of writing which may be distinguished from its communicable content but which in no sense can be subtracted from it: the typographical device can be so subtracted by simple alteration either in the direction of conventional pattern or in the direction of greater distortion. The typography is distinct from style, something superimposed and external to the poem, a mechanical system of variety and a formula of surprise; it is—and this is its function—a psuedo-dynamic feature that galvanizes the imagery with the look of movement, of freedom, of fresh perception, a kind of stylization which is a substitute for a living relation among the images themselves, in the lack of a living relation between the images and the sensibility of the poet. Mr. Cummings' imagery reaches the page still-born.

This characteristic of his verse has been brilliantly analyzed by Mr. R. P. Blackmur, in his "Notes on E. E. Cummings' Language" (*The Hound and Horn*, January, 1931). To that essay I refer the reader for a discussion of Cummings' replacement of stock poetic conventions with an equally limited set of conventions of his own. "By denying the dead intelligence and putting on the heresy of unintelligence," says Mr. Blackmur, "the poet only succeeds in substituting one set of unnourished conventions for another." Again: "As if sensation could be anything more than the idea of sensation . . . without being attached to some central body of experience, genuinely understood and *formed* in the mind." And Mr. Blackmur summarizes his view: "So long as he is content to remain in his private mind, he is unknowable, impenetrable, and sentimental."

These statements reach to the center of Cummings' defects, but I believe that Mr. Blackmur takes too seriously the "heresy of unintelligence"; it is rather the heresy of supposing that personality, as such, outside the terms of something that is not personality, can ever be made known. Now in addition to the typographical mechanism there is another that grows out of it—the mechanism of emotionally private words that are constantly overcharged into pseudo-symbols. This has two aspects. There is the repetition of single words (Mr. Blackmur, in his comprehensive study, examines in detail the personal *clichés*: flower, petal, bloom, etc.); and there is the headlong series of miscellaneous words that attempt to imitate the simultaneity and shock of fresh sensation. Mr. Blackmur shows that the weight of the series cancels the sensory value of its single items. Both this device and the distorted line probably proceed from the poet's sense of the insufficiency of his style: there is something wrong, something obscure that demands a superimposed heightening for effect.

Without this external variety we get, in Cummings, the uniformity that I have mentioned, but it is rather a uniformity of meaning, of reference, than of conception. No single poem introduces the reader to an implicit body of idea beneath its surface, a realm of free play detached once and for all from the poet. We are led to the next poem, and from the aggregate of Mr. Cummings' poems we return to the image of his personality: like all poets he seems to say "more" than the explicit terms convey, but this "more" lies in the origin of the poem, not in the interplay of its own terms. From "To His Coy Mistress" we derive no clue to the existence of such a person as "Andrew Marvell"; from *Viva* we get only the evidence of personality. And this is what Cummings' poetry "means." It is a kind of meaning very common at present; Mr. Cummings is the original head of an easily imitable school. This does not mean that he has ever been *successfully* imitated; no one else has written "personal" poetry as well as Mr. Cummings writes it. It is rather that he has shown the possibility of making personal conventions whose origin and limit are personality. It is a kind of convention that, given "talent," can make of anyone a poet. It requires a certain interest in oneself, which permits one to ascribe to one's "feeling-tone" for words an objective meaning, a comprehensible meaning, to the relations existing among those words. This stanza, by no means an extreme example of pure "feeling-tone," illustrates the process:

> your slightest look easily will unclose me
> though I have closed myself as fingers,
> you open always petal by petal myself as Spring opens
> (touching skilfully, mysteriously) her first rose

There is sententiousness in excess of the occasion, which remains "unknowable," and we are brought back to the poet who becomes the only conceivable reference of an emotion in excess of what is said. But "Cummings" in that sense is an empty abstraction, and the fact that the poet Cummings leads us there, away from the poem itself, explains Mr. Blackmur's remark that the poetry exists only in terms of something that is "impenetrable" and "sentimental." It fails to implicate the reader with the terms of a *formed* body of experience. The poet asks us at last not to attend to the poem as poetry, but to its interesting origin, who, the publisher assures us, has a "cheerful disdain for the approval of pundits and poetasters."

In Mr. Cummings' work there is much to amuse and entertain, and much that one admires. A rigorous selection from his four books would give us some of the best poetry of the age. In & the magnificent sonnet on death and the love sonnet ending "an inch of nothing for your soul," though projected in Mr. Cummings' personal imagery, achieve a measure of objective validity by reference to the traditional imagery of such poetry, which he inverts, but by implication leans upon. His best verse is that in which he succeeds, perhaps unintentionally, in escaping from his own personality into a world of meaning that not even the "heresy of unintelligence" can let him ignore. For this reason he cannot forever be immune to the heavy hand of the pundits. If he finds such pretension tiresome, it is the fate of interesting personalities to be continually bored.

From *Poetry* (March, 1932)

Southern Poetry

EDITORIAL NOTE

THE PURPOSE of this *Southern Number* of POETRY, certainly the editor's purpose, is not to exhibit to the nation a new school of poets, or even to present the work of any new poets at all. And it was far from his intention to show what the South can do in competition with other sections. He has tried merely to get together the best poems by Southern poets he could find at the moment, and to publish some commentary on their present position, intellectually and socially speaking, to the end that the public might draw its own conclusions as to the value of the Southern scene for poetry, and of Southern poets. No other purpose could be defined; a section of this country, which, according to the principles of the Fathers at any rate, is a nation within a nation, is not a definition nor a church with an accessible dogma; it is rather like the features of a face, that can be seen and recognized, and given a denotative name, but not an abstract name. So, in deciding who was entitled to appear in a Southern exhibit, the editor was compelled to rely wholly upon his powers of immediate recognition as the final arbiter over certain other, yet important matters of birth, residence, and even subject-matter. Mr. Archibald MacLeish has written a poem about Mexico, but he is not a Mexican; nor was Shakespeare an Italian. That quality which makes an English poet English similarly makes a writer Southern, or Western, or New England: how long these distinct qualities shall survive, or whether they should survive, are not editorial questions. I refer the reader to Mr. Davidson's essay, printed herein, and to the last paragraph of Mr. Warren's.

The problem is speculative, and although, as Mr. Warren points out, the relation of the poet to his world is an aspect of the significance of scientific ideas in the modern mind, it is probable that it is only an aspect, a more general fashion of stating the oldest problem of esthetics. It is fundamentally the problem of what the poet shall "imitate," and to what end. As poetry grows increasingly abstract, it competes with science, or as Aristotle might have put it, competes with some form of history, and is hence less an imitation of perceived forms than practicable versions of what happens. The local, immediate, and the concrete are the take-off of poetry, and the terms of some long-settled familiarity with concrete features of experience are doubtless the origin of its form. Mr. Ezra Pound has for years belabored the necessity for the concrete, but he seems to give his case away to the scientist in not being able to stop long enough on some few realms of fact to understand them: the result is that the cosmopolitan Mr. Pound, a very great artist, is an incomplete scientist.

The historian of Southern poetry must constantly pause to inquire into the causes of our thin and not very comprehensive performance, in the past, and it may be, as the next generation will see us, in the present also. For the thousands who read William Gilmore Simms' novels and his defense of slavery, a handful knew his poetry, though by any test it deserved as much reading as his prose. There was never a profession of letters in the South. There were, and perhaps here and there there still are, ladies and gentlemen. It is the English social tradition. If there had been a Southern Congreve for a Voltaire to visit, he would have been a "man of fashion" first, or the American synonym for him in the 1840's, and Voltaire would have been disgusted at his lack of professional pride. Perhaps this tradition is still active, but it is certainly less so than it was in the time of Lanier. It may be gone entirely; yet the Southern man of letters, freed from it, has not seen the opportunities of his freedom. On the necessity of making Southern writers, and for that matter American writers, a professional class, bound together by all the ties of a profession whose ethics consists in devotion to the craft—on the need of this, some writer should speedily write a tract, and no title could be better suited to it than *Up from Slavery.*

Yet the problem of professional solidarity is not simple. Society in the United States, in this era, is not more concerned about literature than the plantation was: the plantation did not create a great literature, but it read great literature and it had a profound grasp of ideas relevant to its needs—the only kind of ideas any society ever achieves. The industrialist knows little or nothing, neither imaginative literature nor political philosophy. If the modern writer, unlike the old Southern writer, is emancipated from the demands of social conformity, it is not because he has been intelligently emancipated; it is rather that the decay of social standards has left him free, but nevertheless hanging in the air. The place of the old Southern writer was narrow, it hardly existed, but to the extent that it did exist, it was defined.

Something of this sense of order appears, at least to the editor's mind, to show forth in the poems printed in this issue. (This is partly irrelevant to the question of their merit.) These writers have a point of view: Mr. Percy's sonnet is Victorian, but the "idea" if tame is clearly defined; and Mr. Saville Clark's poetry, which I suppose some persons will find modern and obscure, is equally certain of its terms and point of view. The intellectual problem of the Southern mind is a property spontaneously presented to writers in that section. The historian may say then, that the South now should produce a poetry clearer and more central in its orientation than that of any other American section. That is something to be seen.

It remains to describe the method by which the poets were selected for this issue. They all appear upon invitation; none was asked to *submit* poems—a responsibility that the editor was not in a position to take. Some writers who were asked to contribute, for various reasons could not. Their presence would have given distinction to the exhibit.

To Miss Monroe's sympathetic co-operation with me I cannot express enough gratitude. This number appears in the fortieth volume of Poetry. Each of these volumes attests her eagerness to assist the cause of poetry not only here but abroad; she alone has come from the beginning of the late renascence to the present, with all the vigor of a new start. No single compliment could do justice to her services to the American poet.

From *Poetry* (May, 1932)

Archibald MacLeish

Conquistador, by Archibald MacLeish. Houghton Mifflin Company, 1932.

ALTHOUGH SOME of MacLeish's early poems, notably the first part of "Signature for Tempo," foreshadow the style of *Conquistador*, there is no background in his six previous volumes for the finely sustained tone of the new poem. It is a miniature epic of about two thousand lines: in versification, in diction, in the quality of the narrator's point of view, it stands alone. There is no other poem in English with which as a whole it may be compared. In some specific features of technique which may be isolated but which are, of course, fused with the total quality of the work, *Conquistador* is a production of the school of Ezra Pound. This is no disparagement of MacLeish. For Pound's *Cantos* are full of technical instruction for the poet who knows precisely what he needs to learn. And one either learns something valuable from Pound or misses him altogether. Unlike Eliot, he does not confound the craftsman with his own special moral problems; it is possible to separate the personality from the technical value of the poetry. The school of Eliot gives us something of "lower intensity" than the original; the school of Pound thins out in the aimless exercises of Mr. Dudley Fitts or produces the flawless craft of *Conquistador*.

For a complete history of the conquest of Mexico the reader must go to the historians. The poem is a reconstruction of the part played by one of the lesser heroes, Bernal Diaz del Castillo, who as an old man wrote his reminiscences out of resentment against the official histories by Gomara and the others—

> The quilled professors: the taught tongues of fame:
> What have they written of us: the poor soldiers. . . .

145

> They call the towns for the kings that bear no scars:
> They keep the names of the great for time to stare at—
> The bishops rich men generals cocks-at-arms. . . .

The story is told by Bernal, in flashes of recollection that have enough narrative progression to give the reader variety of scene, but not enough to take his attention from the personality of Bernal and the quality of his character—which is the real subject of the poem. This method disposes of the great modern difficulty of presenting the objective detail of the conventional epic form; the necessity for an external "idea," such as holds the *Aeneid* together, or any sort of cosmic machinery, is likewise dispensed with. We get that peculiarly modern situation: the dramatization of the individual against the background of history. "What have they written of us: the poor soldiers": what can the individual get out of history to sustain him? Nothing appears in the story that Bernal did not see. Everything is enriched by memory. Although Bernal announces his theme as "That which I have myself seen and the fighting," there is little action, for the real subject of the poem is fear at the gradual disappearance of sensation; or, in positive terms, the dramatic quality of the poem consists in the hero's anxiety lest he fail to recover his early life of sensation, upon which his personal identity depends. The meaning of the poem—if we derive and formulate a quality in a general proposition—is the futility of individual action. No man can fully identify the moment of action with the common purpose for which the whole series of events takes place. He is confined to the mechanism of sensation.

For two reasons this "meaning" of *Conquistador* must be emphatically brought out. It will explain its form and it will help to isolate that feature of the style which MacLeish took over from Pound and transformed. And it may lead some of the younger critics to reconsider, not their enthusiasm for the poem, which it richly deserves, but their hasty acceptance of its "philosophy": it is certainly a mistake to suppose that MacLeish has offered a "way out" of the introspective indecision of the school of Eliot, reaffirming a faith in action and heroism against the moral paralysis that the best minds of the older generation seem to have suffered. Not only is there a lack of faith in any kind of action that we might imitate; the poet does not even have much interest in the action implied by the quality of memory that sustains his narrative.

There is not one moment of action objectively rendered in the whole poem. There is constantly and solely the pattern of sensation that surrounds the moment of action. The technique for rendering this special quality is MacLeish's contribution to poetic style, and he has so perfected it that later poets will touch it at the peril of the most slavish imitation:

> Gold there on that shore on the evening sand—
> "Colua" they said: pointing on toward the sunset:
> They made a sign on the air with their solemn
> hands. . . .

> And that voyage it was we came to the Island:
> Well I remember the shore and the sound of that
> place
> And the smoke smell on the dunes and the wind dying:

> Well I remember the walls and the rusty taste of the
> New-spilled blood in the air: many among us
> Seeing the priests with their small and arrogant
> faces. . . .

> Ah how the throat of a girl and a girl's arms are
> Bright in the riding sun and the young sky
> And the green year of our lives where the willows
> are!

This is a new quality in American verse: the clarity of sensuous reminiscence that suffuses the entire poem has appeared in this age only in the prose of Ernest Hemingway, chiefly in the opening pages of *A Farewell to Arms*. Yet the character of the image is derived from Pound:

> Eyes brown topaz,
> Brookwater over brown sand,
> The white hounds on the slope,
> Glide of water, lights and the prore,
> Silver beaks out of night,
> Stone, bough over bough,
> lamps fluid in water,
> Pine by the black trunk of its shadow

And on hill black trunks of the shadow
The trees melted in air.

Pound's image here, as everywhere, is impersonal and objective and timeless, detached from the dramatic context of his own moral position. MacLeish's focus of the image is invariably personal; the image exists only in terms of the character's conception of himself. Its precision has been disciplined in the workshop of Ezra Pound, whose quality of floating clarity is localized in a kind of Browning-esque monologue, in which the moral casuistry is replaced by a highly sophisticated variety of the ancient *chanson de geste*.

The inseparability of image and character brings me to what I believe is a central defect in MacLeish's approach to his subject. It may be stated in moral terms. We cannot linger upon the quality of even the finest passages of the poem without becoming conscious that we are succumbing to a sentimental view of experience. The melancholy of the hero's resentment against the "taught tongues of fame" is obscure and meaningless. It does not at any point emerge as criticism of the avowed pruposes of the "conquest"; and so, instead of a classical irony, we get something like sentimental regret on the part of Bernal, whose anger rises at the failure of the official histories to recreate the sensuous correspondence to his own part in the action. He in effect says not *quorum pars magna fui* but rather *solus quorum omnis fui*—alone in his perceptions. The poem recovers Bernal's perceptions but it does not place them against the objective stream of events. His personal significance is impenetrable; the meaning of the course of outside events is obscure. Bernal's concern is about his personal survival, and he is modern and sentimental; not classical and ironic. The motivation of his story is the fear of death.

It is a little ungrateful to the technical merit of the poem to dwell upon its philosophical limitation, which is deeply rooted in the sensibility of the age. *Conquistador* is one of the perfect examples of that sensibility: for by technical merit I mean the power to sustain the form without a single false note. The verse is *terza rima*, a stanza enormously difficult in English; the paucity of English rhymes ordinarily makes it clumsy and monotonous. But by using in masterly fashion rhyme varied by terminal assonance, which is usually hidden and always cunningly placed, MacLeish rivals the fluent rapidity and ease of the best Italian *terza rima*. It is the first successful example of this stanza in a long English poem. Aside from some of the late Hart Crane's blank verse, it is the only considerable metrical innovation by a poet of this generation. Yet the very perfection of MacLeish's experiment will make future use of *terza rima* dangerous. The technical aspect of the verse is so deeply involved with the quality of MacLeish's sensibility as to be inimitable. "Waller refined our numbers"—but in this case Waller is a hard-pressed modern whose brilliance, once flashed, burns out before it can be passed to other hands. It is the present fate of poetry to be always beginning over again. The kind of "culture" in *Conquistador* is almost purely literary, for the kind of experience in the poem is a sentimentality of spiritual isolation. The almost terrible refinement of the craftsmanship hovers over a void.

From *The New Republic* (June 1, 1932)

Elinor Wylie

Collected Poems of Elinor Wylie, edited by William Rose Benét. Alfred A. Knopf, 1932.

THIS COLLECTION of the verse of Elinor Wylie contains her four volumes exactly as they first appeared and, in addition, forty-seven poems that were not printed in her books. Of these, twenty appear in print for the first time. The book is handsomely bound and beautifully printed, and the editing has been done with great propriety by the poet's husband, Mr. William Rose Benét. Mr. Benét's task was difficult; one is grateful for the restraint and simplicity of his brief memoir, and for the lack on his part of any attempt at criticism.

Although Mrs. Wylie died four years ago—in 1928—and the air of faction that inevitably surrounds a famous poet has lifted, it is still difficult to judge her work. She was both facile and versatile. Her first volume, the book of verse *Nets to Catch the Wind,* appeared in 1921, when she was thirty-four; in the seven years to 1928 she issued three more volumes of poems and four novels. All this work is uneven, and it is hard to select the best of it just because, from first to last, her technical competence permitted her to absorb so many of the literary and moral influences of her time. And I think this same technical mastery kept her, at moments, from ever quite knowing what was her own impulse and what she had assimilated.

It is this feature of her work that explains her brilliant moments and in the end her lack of style: style is that evenness of tone, and permanence of reference for all perceptions, which comes from a mind that, though it may avoid fixed opinions, has nevertheless a

single way of taking hold of its material. And this Mrs. Wylie never
had. The poet who could write, in "Hymn to Earth,"

> A wingless creature heavier than air
> He is rejected of its quintessence;
> Coming and going hence,
> In the twin minutes of his birth and death,
> He may inhale his breath,
> As breath relinquish heaven's atmosphere,
> Yet in it have no share,
> Nor can survive therein
> Where its outer edge is filtered pure and thin:
> It doth but lend its crystal to his lungs
> For his early crying, and his final songs.

—the same poet could write:

> O love, how utterly am I bereaved
> By Time, who sucks the honey of our days,
> Sets sickle to our Aprils, and betrays
> To killing winter all the sun achieved! . . .

One of the defects of Mrs. Wylie's work is that the worst poems
have much of the superficial merit of the best. The worst have invariably a metrical finish, a technical form, a verbal completeness,
that remains hollow inside; the poet did not define her own relation
to the material. This is a problem for the poet at all times, but it is
now peculiarly the modern problem, and one feels that Mrs. Wylie
might have written more solidly in some other age, when the difficulty of self-definition was not so great.

From *The New Republic* (September 7, 1932)

Ezra Pound

How to Read, by Ezra Pound. Desmond Harmsworth, London, 1931.

IN THE BRIEF space of fifty-five pages Mr. Pound discusses the literature of the world, tells us what to read, how to read it, and in the end sets forth a theory of poetry whose novel features will startle his pupils a little less than he may suppose. This book, like most of Mr. Pound's criticism, wears a deceptive simplicity. Perhaps this quality of his prose, admirable in itself, is due to his identification of temperament and thought; he does not distinguish what he has to say from the vehement moral need that he feels of saying it; the simplicity of his literary creed lies not so much in the solution of problems as in his overwhelming sense of the specific problem of the artist. No poet of our age understands this problem so well as Mr. Pound, but one must find the terms in which he understands it. If this small book were all that he had written, it would be difficult to say just what it is he understands: without the supporting evidence of his own great poetry, the theory of poetry offered here would issue stillborn, and fall dead of the inanity of abstraction.

We know that what Mr. Pound understands, as no other living man, is the craftsmanship of verse, and very properly the form that it takes in his verse itself. A decade ago the standard criticism of Mr. Pound was "estheticism," but that cry was irrelevant; he has never been an esthete, he is an artificer; for the esthete is a romantic egoist, while the craftsman may be anything so long as he is aware that his particular art makes certain demands upon him that no other occupation could make. The real criticism of Mr. Pound is not to be directed against his theory as such, but rather at the hasty headlong fashion in which he presents it, at the logical confusion of his intellect when it is not performing the task which is specifically his own, that task being poetry. The justification of Mr. Pound's thesis in *How to Read* is not his arguments, but his poetry.

In his first paragraph he gets started in this fashion:

> When studying physics we are not asked to investigate the biographies of all the disciples of Newton who showed interest in science, but who failed to make any discoveries. Neither are their unrewarded gropings, hopes, passions, laundry bills, or erotic experiences thrust on the hurried student or considered germane to the subject.

From *Part II*:

> Great literature is simply language charged with meaning to the utmost possible degree.

The men who so "charge" language are the "inventors" and the "masters," the latter term being applicable also to the inventors "who, apart from their own inventions, are able to assimilate and co-ordinate a large number of preceding inventions." A third class, "who produce something of lower intensity," are the "diluters." These are the main types of writers, and they represent a division of literature from the point of view of the artist, "independent of the consideration as to whether the passages tend to make the student a better republican, monist, dualist, rotarian, or other sectarian." One must approach the study of poetry as one begins a science: "We proceed by discoveries. We are not asked to memorize the parts of a side-wheeler engine."

This is a naïve piece of false analogy, and I think that Mr. Pound ought to be ashamed of it. In what sense are the great poetical "inventions" similar to scientific "discoveries"? In no sense whatever. A scientific formula refers to an objective process that, theoretically at least, is objectively repeatable. A literary invention is not a formula; it is an accurate rendition of some kind of human experience that may be imitated or combined with other inventions, but none of these imitations or combinations is predictable, or can ever be said to constitute, like the discoveries in physics, a field of knowledge.

What was Mr. Pound driving at when he cooked up so monstrous an abstraction? His classification of the poets is a "true" one, but I think his mistake consists in assuming that the study of the "inventions" exclusively will enable us to invent also. A craftsmanlike attitude towards poetry, which has been dwindling since Dryden, cannot be restored in that way. It is the product of innumerable factors—of the relations among language, church and society, between fathers and mothers, butchers and bakers, between the poet and what society thinks of him. In view of this complication, the laundry bills of Dante should be zealously studied, by somebody like Mr. Pound who would know why he is studying them.

Finally, I should like to intimate that Mr. Pound's own laundry bills might be studied with profit, for they are fuddling his logic. They would make an interesting collection, beginning with Idaho and Indiana, and ending up with the banks of the Susquehanna and the "banks o' Italie." There is Mr. Pound sitting in his heap of miscellaneous laundry bills, so confused outside the moment of his craft (which is the most lucid of our time), that he thinks the laundry bills did the washing: what Mr. Pound needs is just an ordinary Irish or colored washerwoman. To look an honest African wench in the face is better than a column of figures, and is a fine cure for the belief that a poet can get along without having any laundry done at all.

From *Poetry* (November, 1932)

Phelps Putnam

The Five Seasons, by Phelps Putnam. Charles Scribner's Sons, 1931.

THIS SECOND volume of Mr. Putnam's verse contains fourteen poems: twelve new ones and, from *Trinc* (1927), two poems which foreshadowed the larger design of a work that even here is not complete. The new book is the second stage at which the projected work has arrived. It may require many years for completion; meanwhile the hastier and often speciously organized works of less serious poets provide the text for easy commentary that the critics desire. Putnam states no "position"; he offers no "solutions." Although he says that the poems "were conceived in an objective mode," there is at present no promise of an objective design; the poems are fragments from the experience of a kind of picaresque hero who has an insatiable curiosity for American life.

The method that Putnam has chosen, the almost haphazard variety of forms that suggest themselves to him as he proceeds, departs radically from the practice of the leading poets in the last decade. There is no set theme which initiates the reader's mind into the intention of the whole work: each poem is a new event in the hero's life—an event that the poet is willing to present but not to define in too quick an act of understanding. In the case of the late Hart Crane, the symbol of the Brooklyn Bridge was an immediate intuition prior to the perceptions necessary to give it meaning: the final obscurity of *The Bridge* lies in the strain between the arbitrary symbol and the lagging images. Pound's *Cantos* have a similar defect. Simple historical contrast, ancient civilization against modern vulgarity, is a static feat of abstraction that cannot hold the work together. It is a novel theology which argues that the vulgarity of the vulgar constitutes them damned. For no one "experiences" either vulgarity or civilization; they are terms for qualities lying at a depth which Pound does not explore. *The Waste Land* contrasts the present and the past, but these abstract qualities are made properly parallel to the deeper conflict of good and evil which sustains the poem.

In all three of these works the structure which supports their various sorts of obejctive completeness is superimposed on the material. With Pound and Crane it represents a forced conclusion—not the result of long meditation, of long seasoning of the mind in the subject, but rather an assertive act of will that assumes too easily the pretensions of a "philosophy"; meanwhile the disorganized vision of the poet warns us that here, at least, one person has missed salvation. In Eliot's *The Waste Land* the structure—whatever its moral implications may be—is a deliberately chosen convention comparable to the pastoral machinery of "Lycidas." Yet in all these poets a certain generalization precedes the act of writing, a conscious prepossession, dictating the choice of symbols and limiting the poet's range of perception. That is the value of traditional form. Putnam is attempting to construct his work more broadly—tentatively and empirically—with what eventual success no one at present can say. He states no objective in advance either explicitly or through some idea from which we should infer the direction of his work.

All the recent poems, all those, that is, that have been written since the juvenilia in the first part of *Trinc*, set forth the adventures of a group of characters of whom the chief figure is the wanderer Bill Williams. Williams is the "hero"; he alone knows the true nature of his quest—the quest for salvation—and the other characters, Hasbrouck, Smith the poet, Ames, are the partial aspects of his complete sensibility. It is he who asks, in an early poem of the Williams cycle: "What guidance in this mess?" For he is "in hell without a guide." Hell is the modern world, and the ascent from it, the salvation of the hero—in whose salvation, if it is valid, we shall be able to participate—will not be found in quick rationalizations of personal or social crises. It is the mastery of individual experience: Putnam's work began before the Depression and, unaffected by it, it goes its way.

Although Putnam rejects the historical aids to the solution of his problem, he ignores the secular, political view of it now fashionable among the radical Liberals. His concern is his hereditary New England problem of individual integrity, and the search that Williams conducts through hell is for that qualitative and thus indefinable balance of the soul called grace:

> Release me, Lord, now let your child advance
> Into the energy of solitude
> Where there are no fecund murderous paths,
> And wisdom might come beating into me
> Without the need of faulty messengers.

When Bill Williams appears in hell "without a guide," we know that the Vergilian intellect, or the wisdom of the past, is powerless to explain his plight; the intellect is a faulty messenger. In the midst of hell, or suddenly, perhaps elsewhere, but without knowing that he has escaped, Williams glimpses heaven—sees for a moment the tortured grace that he pursues; but—

> At the top of heaven I remembered hell . . .

And:

> My Lord, must I still suffer memory?

Heaven and hell are not clearly divided; the emotions of the hero are mixed. This explains, I believe, the lack of internal form in many of the poems, chiefly in the magnificently written "Daughters of the Sun." That poem is an invocation of the sun as a religious symbol, but its religious properties are not common knowledge, and are unknown also to the hero who speaks the prayer. The result is that no objective emotions are established to which the hero can return for illumination of his experience, past or to come. The sun does not reach the fixation of a symbol, and the hero's complex emotions remain at the end in their initial state of complication. They have not attached themselves to a fixed meaning; the hero moves on, "suffering memory" of his emotions. He derives nothing from the past; and so, in the "Hymn to Chance," he prays to the god of modern disorder:

> Make us tough and mystical,
> Give us such eyes as will penetrate your eyes
> And lungs to draw the breath you give to us.
> Hear us for we do not beg;
> We only pray you heal our idiot ways
> The kind of lonely madness which we have
> Of bleeding one another on the road.
> We travel in the belly of the wind;
> It is you, Lord, who will make us lame or swift.

The blurring out of the imagery in the fifth, sixth, and seventh lines reveals the chief defect of Putnam's work, and betrays at the same time the limitations of this sort of poetic empiricism. "Bleeding one another on the road" is a simple statement whose fundamental obscurity lies in the tentative character of the supporting symbolism of the whole work. Its possible justification is its relation to a sensibility that contemporary eyes cannot discern—a sensibility that may, as in the case of Baudelaire, be recognized later as one of the deepest of the age.

Bill Williams' empiricism, his refusal to take any provisional advice from the fragmentary wisdom of the past, suggests that for the present at least he may be more interested in having his adventures, in suffering the memory of their intensity, than in understanding them. We must remember that he is first of all an American hero; he must be tough enough to withstand the shock of new experience; mystical, that is to say, sceptical enough to test all the experience of his age before he is willing to settle down.

However, one may suspect that Putnam's determination to make his hero's religion a brand new one, his unwillingness to keep an open mind about the past, his intolerance of the ideas, symbols, terms of other times, is due to a rebellion of one side of his intelligence that has subtly affected all sides of it. In the positive search of Williams for the state of grace, there is the negative revolt against the narrow exclusion of the sensuous life from the New England mind. This leads him in many of the poems to imagine the state of grace in terms of sexual pleasure; it is an ancient metaphor, but Putnam's use of it is literal. The two ecstasies are identical; the glimpse of heaven from the depths of hell is a moment's sensation; then it is all hell again in an inconclusive irony that takes the hero no forwarder in his quest.

It is a curious fact that the discovery of the sensuous world by New England writers often turns out to be a rediscovery of sex. Then follows an excitement of revolt. Henry Adams reconstructed the thirteenth century out of his impulse to find a rich world of sense, and the impulse carried with it the necessity to conduct his search in moral terms: when sensuousness and morality are added together (in New England) the sum is woman, and we get from Adams the abstraction, Nature is moral contingency—the perfect symbol of which, for his devious and snobbish intelligence, was the Virgin of Chartres. Mr. Robinson's heroes dry up in a world of deliquescent senses; they commit murder and adultery, at times even rape; but they never move easily in the sensuous world, and they never seem to feel any of their crimes—which they talk about thirty years later.

In the first poem of this volume, "Words of An Old Woman," Putnam makes the American soil speak its bitterness against the lust of power. "The hero, Bill Williams, had for a while the notion that he was in search of power": the Old Woman gives him a new object—the search for a religious conception of Man in Nature. Nature has been raped; the lust of power has destroyed man's easy access to the sensuous world; it has reduced his position in it to a pragmatic abstraction. Where shall we satisfy the need of the religious mind for contemplation, whose sole power is power over oneself? That is the question that Putnam is asking—a question to which he will not give a hasty answer. For the answer is not a formula; it must come out of the way in which men live. These poems are rare evidence of a poet's patience and integrity in that most thankless of his tasks—the re-creation of the whole image of man.

From *Hound and Horn* (January–March, 1933)

Stephen Spender

Poems, by Stephen Spender. Faber & Faber, 1933.

MR. STEPHEN SPENDER'S book contains thirty-three poems that will have a distinct influence upon his contemporaries, not only in England but, I believe, in the United States where for the last twenty years the best verse in the English language has been written. Mr Spender's originality though limited is genuine; his range as yet is slight but his quality is not surpassed by any other English poet since the war. For one thing, he has not been compelled to circumvent Eliot in order to speak for himself. Within the general terms of the intellectual crisis of the age, Spender has defined a personal crisis of his own; he begins a solution of the problem in the only way that art is capable of solutions—by giving the problem a fundamental restatement. There is a danger, however, that the meaning of this quality in Spender's work will be missed for a time: his faults will certainly be imitated, his "philosophy" (as such) mistaken for his style, and a kind of rambling accumulation of sensitive perceptions (see poem xxxii) will become the latest mode of Communist verse.

It is one of the defects of revolutionary thought, in this age, so far as poetry is concerned, that it is not assimilable to any great body of sensuous forms. It was possible for Shelley to imagine, at least, that he was rewriting the classical mythology. Our own contemporaries have the gospel according to Father Marx, certain passages of which are almost as moving as Dickens; most of it is merely engaging dialectically, leaving the young humanitarian to flounder in an opaque mass of abstraction that is not easily translated into the mere physical objects that the distressed Platonist, in all times, is com-

160

pelled to see. The raw initiate into the Society of Friends would suffer, as poet, a similar disability. In the case of Mr Spender, there is a tendency to work out his philosophy as he goes along, as if he were making a literal translation of the doctrine into metaphors:

> The architectural gold-leaved flower
> From people ordered like a single mind,
> I build.

Or this:

> . . . larger than all the charcoaled batteries
> And imaged towers against that dying sky,
> Religion stands, the church blocking the sun.

Such translation probably precedes the creative moment, and the best poetry is probably written by men who are not even aware that it has taken place: the actual expression is the total thought. In these passages, Mr Spender oscillates between two social relatives that have imposed upon him as poetic absolutes. The verse is didactic and as dead as Blackmore and Ambrose Phillips. As social and political men we may, if we choose, select all the provisional absolutes that we desire; as poets we must be selected by some absolute. We may then criticize it or even reject it, but we cannot get rid of it; like Lord Tennyson's God, it is nearer than hands and feet.

If there is a single good dogma in poetic criticism it is possibly this: that no philosophy is good enough for a poet unless it is so seasoned in his experience that it has become, like the handling of the gravediggers' skulls, a property of easiness. It is not what a poet "believes" (Mr Richards' theory) but rather what total attitude he takes towards all aspects of his conduct, that constitutes the "content" side of the aesthetic problem. Belief is a statistical and sociological category as applied to the arts: does the poet believe in the trinity? does he believe in votes for women? There may be an equally good theory that modern poets believe entirely too much—that is to say, more than they can, as poets, understand. One might derive from this slender volume more specific beliefs than from the whole of the *Divine Comedy*, in which "belief" in Mr Richards' sense of the term does not appear.

It is not necessary to give to Mr Spender's philosophy a name; it has been necessary to describe its function in his work, in order to clear the ground. All his best poems convey *single emotions*. And these single emotions are created, in the sense that a table or a chair is created; they are not believed. Poem xiv ("In 1929") is one of the best, possibly the best in the book, and certainly one of the finest English poems of the century. These lines possess an absolute clarity, a complete mastery of words, that has been absent from English verse since Landor (Mr Spendor's metrics deserves separate discussion: he has obviously studied the later Yeats, but without trying to become Yeats):

> Now I suppose that the once envious dead
> Have learnt a strict philosophy of clay
> After these centuries, to haunt us no longer
> In the churchyard or at the end of the lane
> Or howling at the edge of the city
> Beyond the last beanrows, near the new factory.

It is this quality that should influence the contemporary scene.

From *New Verse* (May, 1933)

Edwin Arlington Robinson

Talifer, by Edwin Arlington Robinson. The Macmillan Company, 1933.

EDWIN ARLINGTON ROBINSON, the most famous of living American poets, was born at Head Tide, Maine, on December 22, 1869. He attended Harvard from 1891 to 1893, but left college without being graduated. In 1896 he printed privately his first book of verse, *The Torrent and the Night Before,* which was followed a year later by *The Children of the Night,* a volume little noticed at the time but one which marks the beginning of a new era in American poetry. In the next fourteen years he published two more books, *Captain Craig* (1902) and *The Town Down the River* (1910); but it was not until 1916 that he attracted attention and first attained to a notable fame. For with *The Man Against the Sky,* Mr. Robinson stepped quickly into the front rank of American verse. In the earlier years of his career he wrote some of the finest lyrics of modern times: these are likely to become the foundation of his permanent claim to fame.

The new volume, *Talifer,* is a psychological narrative of the order of *Captain Craig;* it is the eighth or ninth specimen of this type of work that Mr. Robinson has given us. Because the type has grown thinner with each new example, the new narrative being, I believe, the least satisfactory of them all, it is the occasion of some inquiry into the causes of Mr. Robinson's preference for this particular form. It is a form that includes the three Arthurian poems, *Merlin, Lancelot,* and *Tristram,* psychological stories that are in all respects similar to the New England tales of Nightingale, Cavender, Bartholow. All is the same but the time and place; for the characters are the same.

In *Talifer* there are four characters, two men and two women. The woman Althea—the name is a dry piece of humorous abstraction—is in love with Talifer; she is woman domestic and sensitive but commonplace and child-bearing. Talifer himself is an ordinary man, but he talks of his "tradition," carries himself well, and expects of life more than his inner quality entitles him to: so he imagines that he is in love with the other woman, Karen, who is beautiful, treacherous, cold and erudite, dividing her time between inscrutable moods and incredible reading in the ancients. She is vaguely conceived by the poet, so that the entire motivation of the hero's action remains obscure. Talifer is fatuous enough to say that with Karen he expects to find Peace. Life becomes, after a year or two with her, intolerable. Then, one day in his ancestral forest, he meets Althea (who still loves him), and he decides to leave Karen. Now all this time, the other man, Doctor Quick, could have been in love with either of the women; he is too skeptical to push his desires; and his role in the drama is that of commentator. He explains the action to the other characters, and affords to the poet a device by which the real actors become articulate. The story ends with the reappearance, after a couple of years, of Quick: in the meantime Talifer has married Althea, who has a child. Although Quick himself had tried to participate in life by taking Karen off to a "cottage in Wales," his return testifies to his failure. But he is not much affected by it. He proceeds to analyze for Althea and Talifer the true basis of their love, which is thoroughly commonplace after a good deal of romantic pretense.

Mr. Robinson's style in the new poem is uniform with the style of its predecessors: it is neither better nor worse than the style of *The Glory of the Nightingales* or of *Cavender's House*. It requires constant reviewing by Mr. Robinson's admirers to keep these poems distinct; at a distance they lose outline and blur into one another. They really constitute a single complete poem that the poet has not succeeded in writing, a poem of which these indistinct narratives are partial formulations.

We get, in them all, a character doomed to defeat—or a character who, when the tale opens, is a failure in the eyes of his town, but who wins a secret moral victory, as in *The Man Who Died Twice*. But Talifer, whose conceit betrays him into an emotional life that he cannot understand, is not quite defeated. The tragic solution of his problem being rejected by Mr. Robinson, and replaced by a somewhat awkward bit of domestic irony, Talifer at first sight appears to be a new kind of Robinsonian character. Yet the novelty, I think, lies merely in the appearance. For Talifer is the standard Robinsonian character grown weary of his tragic role, accepting at last the fact that his tilt at fate had less intensity than he supposed, and

> with grateful ears
> That were attuned again to pleasant music
> Heard nothing but the mellow bells of peace.

That is the end of the poem.

I have remarked that the character of Karen is vaguely conceived, with the result that Talifer's relationship with her lacks motivation. Those mellow bells of peace are therefore a little hollow in sound, for their ring is as inexplicable as the noisy chaos of the erudite Karen, upon whose prior significance they entirely depend. The plot, in brief, lacks internal necessity. And the domestic peace of the conclusion remains arbitrary, in spite of Mr. Robinson's efforts through his mouthpiece, Doctor Quick, to point it up with some sly irony at the end. The irony is external—as if Mr. Robinson had not been able to tell the story for what it was, and had to say: This is what life is really like, a simple wife and a child—while ring those bells of peace that would be tiresome if one had more sense.

Mr. Robinson's genius is primarily lyrical; that is to say, he seldom achieves a success in a poem where the idea exceeds the span of a single emotion. It is, I think, significant that his magnificent poem "The Mill" is highly dramatic, whereas the whole range of his narrative verse yields but a few moments of drama that are swiftly dispersed by the dry casuistry of the commentary upon them. The early "Richard Cory" is s perfect specimen of Mr. Robinson's dramatic powers—when those powers are lyrically expressed; similarly "Luke Havergal" is one of the finest lyrics of modern times.

It is most probable that the explanation of the popular success of *Tristram*, and of most of the Robinson narratives, lies in the loss of the dramatic instinct by the contemporary public. It is a loss increasingly great since the rise of middle-class comedy in the eighteenth century. Instead of the tragic hero whose downfall is deeply involved with his supra-human relations, we get the romantic, sentimental hero whose problem is chiefly one of adjustment to society, on the one hand, and, on the other, one of futile self-assertion in the realm of the personal ego. Mr. Robinson's Talifer exhibits both these phases of the modern sensibility: he plays with his ego in the irrational marriage with Karen, and he later sees his difficulty strictly in terms of a social institution, or of social adjustment, in the second marriage with Althea (who, of course, represents "truth"). The dramatic approach to the situation that Mr. Robinson set for his story is put aside; for the dramatic approach would have demanded the possession, by the hero, of a comprehensive moral formula. He would have applied this formula with extreme rigor to his total conduct, with the result that it would have broken down somewhere and thrown the hero into tragic consequences, from which it would be impossible for him to escape. The story as it is told is hardly more than anecdotal; Mr. Robinson turns his plot, at the end, into a commonplace joke about the deliquescent powers of marriage on the pretensions of human nature.

It is one of the anomalies of contemporary literature that Mr. Robinson, who has given us a score of great lyrics, should continue to produce these long narrative poems, one after another, until the reader can scarcely tell them apart. We may guess at the reason for this. Our age provides for the poet no epos or myth, no pattern of well understood behavior, which the poet may examine in the strong light of his own experience. For it is chiefly those times that prefer one kind of conduct to another, times that offer to the poet a seasoned code, which have produced the greatest dramatic literature. Drama depends for clarity and form upon the existence of such a code. It matters little whether it is a code for the realization of good, like Antigone's; or a code for evil like Macbeth's. The important thing is that it shall tell the poet how people try to behave, and that it shall be too perfect, whether in good or in evil, for human nature. The poet seizes one set of terms within the code—for example, feudal ambition in *Macbeth*—and shows that the hero's application of the code to his own conduct is faulty, and doomed to failure. By adhering strictly to the code, the poet exhibits a typical action, and if he is a Shakespeare he exhibits it with finality. But Mr. Robinson has no epos, myth or code to tell him what the terminal points of human conduct are, in this age; so he goes over the same ground, again and again, writing a poem that will not be written.

It has been pointed out by T. S. Eliot that the best lyric poetry of our time is dramatic, that it is good because it is dramatic. It is a tenable notion that the dramatic instinct, after the Restoration and down to our own time, survived best in the lyric poets. With the disappearance of general patterns of conduct, the power to depict action that is both *single* and *complete* also disappears. The dramatic genius of the poet is held to short flights, and the dramatic situation is a fragment of a total action which the poet lacks the means to delineate. It is to be hoped that Mr. Robinson will again exercise his dramatic genius where it has a chance for success: in lyrics.

From *The New Republic* (October 25, 1933)

John Peale Bishop

Now With His Love, by John Peale Bishop. Charles Scribner's Sons, 1933.

THERE IS no more distinguished work in modern poetry than "Ode," "The Return," "The Ancestors," "Perspectives Are Precipices"; perhaps "In the Dordogne," "Twelfth Night" and "Beyond Connecticut, Beyond the Sea" should be added to the list: a formidable exhibit to appear in a first volume. But the book is long overdue; Mr. Bishop has been the most interesting unpublished poet of his generation. The poems that I have named show little or no trace of the influence of Eliot, Pound and Yeats, who largely dominate the early poems in the volume. But it is significant that Bishop should include the early poems. By studying the styles of the earlier masters he learned the meaning of artistic limitations; on the negative side this book is an enchiridion of the poetic styles that the ideas and emotions of the age brought to the front; and it is by discipline in these styles that Bishop has emerged into a poetry of his own. He has given us the record.

The best work, to which I have called attention, has a remarkable feature. But for a single trace of "Gerontion" they are all free of influence; yet they are all written in different "styles" (a similar type of free verse appears in several of the poems, but the imagery and phrasing point to no one center of interest). Each poem creates a new problem asking for a new solution. Bishop has not found a characteristic style that he can impose upon the great variety of his material. It is not necessarily a defect but, defect or not, the explanation of this anomaly would define a sort of poetry new in our time and would possibly set limits to its later achievement.

There is, then, the contemporary preoccupation with styles (not

168

simply style), with metrical forms, and with the structure of the line. But Bishop, of all the modern poets who take this approach, feels the least uneasiness about a proper subject matter. There is no one subject, no one scene, nor a single kind of imagery coming from a single subject or scene: every poem as I say, is a new problem. And Bishop feels no inhibitions in the presence of any kind of material. It is a new turn in the modern metaphysical school. But there is a distinct danger in it even for a fine technician like Bishop. Where a weaker poet would run into incoherence or sentimentality, Bishop gives us a neat piece of refinement or dandyism: it is in this phase of his work alone that the personality is not secondary to the work, for here the personality must take the place of a complete mastery of a realm of experience. There is not that overwhelming possession of a subject whose meaning can never be divorced from its sensuous presentation, which we get in such different poets as Hardy and Eliot.

There is the great variety of eclectic subjects. Alongside these, there is a philosophical bias—subordinate in the slighter pieces; in the better, driving the material into significance (see "Easter Morning") and, in the best work, shading finely off into the subject so that we get neither thesis nor impression, but the fusion of both in a genuine poetry.

In this, again, lies the modern dilemma. If Bishop does not solve it, he points to a temporary direction that we may take. The poet must see the totality of experience, not statistically or geographically (which is the way that sociological poets have of being anti-social); he must see it freshly and innocently wherever he may be. It is the realization of this, doubtless, that has put Bishop to some extent under the influence of certain modern painters, who offer the pure object without peril of philosophy. So the problem is to bring to bear upon the object a philosophical point of view that shall in the end be lost in the object itself; it is only what the best poetry of all ages has done when it has avoided excessive refinement on the one hand, and, on the other, a facile didacticism. These are the two risks that Bishop in the future must run; though I suspect that the toughness and incredulity of his point of view will preserve him from the facility at least. He is dominated by a settled view of the nature of man which is essentially religious, and is committed to the "classical" belief that poetry must look at man under the head of eternity.

How this shall be done is another way of stating the modern problem. If the "social" point of view can subdue the philosophy to the material, and close the disjunction between experience and form, power and ritual, the literature of the future belongs to that point of view; but it will be a nice question then whether it will still be the social point of view. There is no evidence that this will happen; for communist poetry at present is an aggravated case of one symptom of the right-wing disease—the "heresy of the didactic," which the communists undertake as enthusiastically as their opponents deplore it. We are now all necessarily moralists. Apart from the great distinction of the poetry in this book, Bishop has shown us once more the fundamentals of the art and the way they must be recovered.

> But He is dead
> Christ is dead. And in a grave
> Dark as a sightless skull He lies
> And of his bones are charnels made.

Of this didacticism Bishop knows the cure:

> The ceremony must be found
> Traditional, with all its symbols.

From *The New Republic* (February 21, 1934)

Mark Van Doren

A Winter Diary and Other Poems, by Mark Van Doren. The Macmillan Company, 1935.

LET IT BE said at the beginning that Mr. Van Doren's chief defect as a poet seems to be his ease of expression. It is, I think, justly suspect in this age; but to understand it one must remember the age of Dryden, when poetry was not scrutinized closely for its high moments; it was an objective art with the properties of rhyme and meter, and an expected level of diction as well. It was not a specific kind of experience. Any kind of experience could go into it; the whole range of thought and feeling, from emotion at high tension to casual observation, naturally went into verse.

Mr. Van Doren's poetry is of this order, and I think it is necessary to bear the point in mind before we can even begin to decide how good the work is. If we are suspicious of a mellifluous tongue, we are suspicious because poetry is no longer an objective art; we are not satisfied with a mere high level of technical performance; we deny that the properties of such a performance have any force of themselves, or that the means of the performance, taken alone, exist.

This is all very well; but let us glance at what Mr. Van Doren has actually done in four volumes of miscellaneous poems and in one long narrative. I believe that *Jonathan Gentry* received its due from one reviewer. I do not mean that other persons did not praise it; simply that Miss Marianne Moore alone saw in it a sustained mastery of narrative style that is said to be impossible today. The three volumes, *Spring Thunder*, *7 P.M.*, and *Now the Sky*, contain, to our modern taste, much that is negligible. But it should be remembered

171

that they contain nothing that is bad. And they do contain a great deal of poetry that is sound and distinguished.

We are not to suppose that Mr. Van Doren is the kind of poet who does not know his own best work; who needs an editor or asks his reader to edit him. It is rather that the indifferent bulk of his verse points to an approach to his material that is a necessary condition of his best level. He is the only serious poet in this country who is able to apply constantly, without the unease of the social and historical mind, a single and remarkably pure sensibility to a medium that he is able to take on the whole for granted.

From the three earlier books of shorter poems I could select twenty that are among the best contemporary examples of poetry. From the new volume I should select about eight. Of no other poet in his generation could more be expected.

The title poem of the present volume, for all its sensitive observation, its sustained tone, and its clarity of outline, seems to me to suffer the disability of most long poems of our time: it has temporal progression from scene to scene, but it has little dramatic force. It is a lyrical impulse extended and thinned out in a chronological outline that is not, properly speaking, form. The same may be said of "The Eyes"—which, like "Winter Diary," contains some of Mr. Van Doren's best writing—where the main symbolism runs off at the end into mere statement, a blurring of image that leaves the conclusion in the air.

The distinguished section of the book is "Return to Ritual." These fifteen poems are a volume within a volume that I commend to the meditation of persons who demand of a poet, in his successive books, "growth" and ever some further novelty of style. In his best work over a period of ten years Mr. Van Doren has not "grown"; his style is essentially what it was in 1924. In "Why Sing at All"—

> So will the vales be green,
> And joy and desire stand up, and pride start growing

the general statement is not conceived in terms of anything that the poem allows us to know; it is a kind of statement that Mr. Van Doren did not permit himself in the early books; and if it is growth, it is to be deplored. But that he has grown in another sense, that he has steadily mastered a form that may be termed, I believe, the psychological lyric, and mastered it without any alteration of his original direction, cannot be denied. He is akin to Robinson in this, but not derivative of Robinson. In "This Amber Sunstream" the setting sun throws its slanting ray into a room; this is the last stanza:

> Another hour and nothing will be here.
> Even upon themselves the eyes will close.
> Nor will this bulk, withdrawing, die outdoors
> In night, that from another silence flows.
> No living man in any western room
> But sits at amber sunset round a tomb.

The poem is, I think, the high moment of the book. It should be read, of course, as a whole, many times. It belongs to no school; it offers no exciting new method to poets younger than Mr. Van Doren; it presents a common emotion in new but not startling terms, out of that common center of the language that few modern poets are able to master; and in the bald simplicity of diction the poet achieves an elegance of tone that cannot be explained as conscious style.

After this poem, it is, I fear, a little ungracious to discard all but a handful of Mr. Van Doren's thirty-four sonnets. Sonnet XXI is distinguished; three or four others reward careful study. But is not the sonnet inherently a romantic form? It states a crisis; the emotion is defined by means of counter-statement; this, at least, is the method of Shakespeare, who must be our standard. As I have said, Mr. Van Doren has a limpidity and an ease that long ago ceased to be general features of poetry; perhaps we should not ask him, a meditative poet, to sustain a long dramatic sequence of sonnets. But we shall continue to demand of him the kind of poetry that we find in "This Amber Sunstream." We cannot decide absolutely how good it is; but if it is good, it is clear that it will be as good in 1980 as it is today.

From *The Nation* (March 20, 1935)

Baudelaire in Translation

Flowers of Evil. From the French of Charles Baudelaire. By George Dillon and Edna St. Vincent Millay. Harper and Brothers, 1936.

THE FAULTS of these translations might have been fewer and less serious had Miss Millay and Mr. Dillon used pentameter instead of the hexameter of the French. Not that they do not often succeed in writing good hexameters: Miss Millay particularly avoids placing the caesura so that it breaks the line into two trimeters—or a tetrameter with two feet dangling at the end. In this difficulty both translators have been ingenious; but space does not allow citations of a special competence, the brilliance of which seems to me to be irrelevant to the task of translating Baudelaire. Miss Millay says in her preface that part of her task was to make the English sound like French verse. One cannot argue with this, but one may suppose that if the translation is still French it is not English, that it is only half-translated.

French words are longer than English words; so the trouble with Baudelaire in English hexameters is that whoever does the job is likely to put into the English a good deal that was not in the French. The line, "Je veux, pour composer chastement mes églogues," is rendered by Mr. Dillon: "I want to write a book of chaste and simple verse"—eleven words for seven, an adverb weakened into an adjective, and another adjective put in, the whole effect being blurred. Let us see what Mr. Dillon does to the first stanza of "Réversibilité":

> Ange plein de gaîté, connaissez-vous l'angoisse,
> La honte, les remords, les sanglots, les ennuis
> Et les vagues terreurs de ces affreuses nuits
> Qui compriment le cœur comme un papier qu'on froisse . . .

Mr. Dillon:

> Spirit of happiness, hast thou heard tell of woe?
> Hast thou heard tell of anguish, and remorse, and care—
> Of those long nights when in the black fist of Despair
> The heart is crumpled up like paper? . . .

Ange is not "spirit." *Gaité* is not "happiness." *Connaissez-vous* is not "hast thou heard tell of"; but Mr. Dillon needed two more syllables for his hexameter than the simple "Do you know" would have allowed him; so we get the lofty "hast thou" combined with "heard tell of"—a mixed style that turns Baudelaire over in his grave. (Baudelaire frequently combines Racinian rhetoric and the common phrase, but not in this passage.) In the second line the exigencies of English hexameter compel Mr. Dillon to repeat "Hast thou heard tell"; he needs some rapid monosyllables that will maintain the nearly accentless movement of the French; but he is also compelled to break up the emphasis of the original. He breaks the flow of the original by making the first line a unit, end-stopped: *angoisse*, coming first in the series of griefs, is the most abstract and it sets the "tone"; it is followed dramatically by the concrete varieties of grief. The series culminates with *terreurs*, but Mr. Dillon violates it by substituting "long nights," which is not a coordinate term. Baudelaire's list of the afflictions of human nature rises to a powerful climax in the subtle figure of suffocation (*compriment le coeur*) which is suddenly illuminated with marvelous accuracy by means of the simile of the crumpled paper. Mr. Dillon runs it all together in an undergraduate metaphor of his own, which exaggerates out of existence the effect achieved by Baudelaire.

I have labored one point about a stanza that I selected at random. There are passages, even whole poems, in which Mr. Dillon is more successful; there are passages and poems in which Miss Millay is more successful than Mr. Dillon ever is. Here is Miss Millay's beginning for one of the great poems:

> The child, in love with globes and maps of foreign parts,
> Finds in the universe no death and no defect . . .

—which is not bad in itself; but it is not Baudelaire:

> Pour l'enfant, amoureux de cartes et d'estampes,
> L'univers est égal à son vaste appétit . . .

This is neither good nor Baudelaire:

> Oh, Death, old captain, hoist the anchor! Come, cast off!
> We've seen this country, Death! We're sick of it! Let's go!
>
> O Mort, vieux capitaine, il est temps! levons l'ancre
> Ce pays nous ennuie, O Mort! Appareillons!)

The formal invocation of *O Mort* is converted into an expression of personal emotion—"Oh, Death." In English one does not hoist anchor. Nor can one begin to render the passage until one has understood the force of *il est temps!* without which one of the great passages of nineteenth-century verse would be commonplace. Miss Millay omits it. If *Appareillons!* is untranslatable, it is surely not "Let's go!" It is astonishing to see how much that is wrong Miss Millay gets out of *Ce pays nous ennuie!*

Mr. Dillon's version of "Lesbos" is his best contribution to the book, though here as elsewhere he puts in his own pretty adjectives that give Baudelaire something of a Junior League tone. Miss Millay is at her best, I think, in her rendering of "L'Imprévu." Nothing in this book equals James Elroy Flecker's version of "Don Juan aux Enfers," or Aldous Huxley's "Femmes Damnées." This difficult poem the present translators do not attempt. They give us fewer than half of *Les Fleurs du Mal*; so a fairer title for their book would have been *Selections from Baudelaire*. The translations by F. P. Sturm, in the Modern Library, will give the reader without French a better introduction to the poet than the more "creative" performance of Mr. Dillon and Miss Millay. Sturm is only a versifier, but he has his eye on Baudelaire; he leaves out a good deal, but he puts in very little of his own.

From *The Nation* (July 4, 1936)

R. P. Blackmur and Others

Salt Water Ballads, by Robert P. Tristram Coffin. The Macmillan Co.
Address to the Living, by John Holmes. Henry Holt and Co.
They Say the Forties, by Howard Mumford Jones. Henry Holt and Co.
The Emperor Heart, by Laurence Whistler. The Macmillan Co.
Darkling Plain, by Sara Bard Field. Random House.
Poems, by C. F. MacIntyre. The Macmillan Co.
Monticello and Other Poems, by Lawrence Lee. Charles Scribner's Sons.
The Sleeping Fury, by Louise Bogan. Charles Scribner's Sons.
From Jordan's Delight, by R. P. Blackmur. Arrow Editions.

IN THE NINE books before me for this quarter's commentary there are two that contain verse that rises above the level of competent "period style." These two books are by Miss Bogan and Mr. Blackmur, but if a few brilliant passages are enough to redeem an otherwise merely good performance, perhaps there is a third volume: Mr. Lawrence Lee's. Three months cannot represent a period, nor even a year; nor could the books of a year represent a period, or even a decade. There is nevertheless in the poets of this quarter no indication that seven years of the 1930's have witnessed discoveries peculiar to the present decade: even Mr. Blackmur's poetry is a brilliant consolidation of the gains made by his predecessors of the 'twenties, and Miss Bogan is only better than she was ten years ago, not different. There is no reason why Miss Bogan or Mr. Blackmur, since they are good, should be different from their previous selves or anybody else. But the younger poets represented here are singularly unenterprising: while they are under no obligation to give us brand-new styles, if their immediate past affords them a satisfactory starting-point, they ought at least to examine closely what they have had handed on to them: they have sat down very quickly and eaten it up.

Just ten years ago Riding and Graves, in *A Survey of Modernist Poetry*, a book that has been grossly neglected, made this illuminating statement: "The whole trend of modern poetry is toward treating poetry like a very sensitive substance which succeeds better when allowed to crystallize by itself than when put into prepared moulds: this is why modern criticism, deprived of its discussions of questions of form, tries to replace them by obscure metaphysical reflections." It is a judgment that applies to criticism as a whole today, with honorable exceptions in the direction of Mr. Winters, Mr. Ransom, and Mr. Blackmur himself. For the Marxists and the Humanists have only seemed to make the metaphysical reflections less obscure by making them crude, and they have got rid of the sensitive substance only by substituting for it a dogmatic subject matter. The technical analysis of verse is no forwarder today—with the honorable exceptions that have not yet affected the popular reviewers—than it was in the age of free-verse.

The poetry of our time must inevitably suffer from this lack, though it would be rash to assume that a more rigorous criticism, ten years ago, would have made it harder for our inferior poets to write: it would have made it considerably harder for them to write today as Messrs. Coffin, Holmes, and Jones do, in facile reproductions of certain "period styles" of the middle 'twenties. Mr. Coffin, with some degree of tenacious humility, has made of Mr. Frost's a period style; Mr. Holmes has taken Stephen Vincent Benet's "style," made it hortatory and wholesome, spiritually problemed and "American"; and Mr. Jones—alas, what can be said of Mr. Howard Mumford Jones? But Mr. Jones may speak for himself:

> O great white Christ, beautiful and compassionate,
> Thou who takest away the sins of the world,
> Thou clean bright sword, thou pillar, thou banner unfurled
> At morning, imperial and importunate,
> Thou symbol beyond all creeds, all forms of state,
> Thou from whose face corruption and lust are swirled
> Into nothingness, whose strong fingers are curled
> About the earth, upholding it—though we come late
> Into an evil time, and though decay

> Has been our father, and despair our mother,
> Though our hearts are set hard against thee, and our lips
> Deny thee, and we have scourged thee again with whips,
> Who art our victim and our torture and our brother,
> We cry unto thee from the blood and tears of this day.

It is not so much period style as period sentiment. The time is rather too easily evil, decay and despair an ancestry a little too fashionable, and altogether Christ is too various and stagy and the blood and tears a little too much the rabbits out of the hat, to convince us that Mr. Jones is not really spoofing us. I trust that it is not necessary to go far into this matter. Whose blood and tears? Where did they come from? . . . Mr. Jones prefers the sonnet, but he occasionally gives us a lyric, and here is the last stanza of "You That Were Beautiful":

> You that were wonderful,
>   Where have you gone,
> Whose breast of ivory
>   Like silver shone?

But the style of the poets in Godey's *Lady's Book* alternates with the styles of Eliot and of Cummings. Eliot: "When the arteries harden, a picture, a phrase, a face?/Shall I tell them the bitter truth? Would it be worthwhile?" Cummings: ". . . the din/of female voices lifts and explodes above/the sudden sandwiches . . . " Among the female voices would it be worthwhile to remind Mr. Jones that for years he has held up Eliot as an excellent example of fraud? I am at a loss to understand why the amusing verse in this book—a kind of harsh *vers de société*, as if the late Calvin Coolidge had stooped to the *genre*—comes right out of Eliot, while the notes piped in other strains sound like the magazine verse of eighty years ago, a period style not quite in tune with the Eliot-Cummings era. Couldn't Mr. Jones have used, for his *vers de société*, a model a little nearer in time to Godey's? There was William Mackworth Praed, good enough for anybody.

If I have been hard on Mr. Jones, I can only plead in defense the mild discouragement of a reader who has looked for a reason why this verse should have been written, and looked in vain. Mr. Jones will amuse us for a few lines, then get serious, or worse, and bathetic. In sonnet V of *The Forties*, a sequence about modern disillusionment, in which Eliot, Hemingway, and Faulkner are blamed for a good deal of Mr. Jones' woe, there is a kind of scramble of allusions which appear only to remind us that Mr. Jones has read Shakespeare, Donne, and Keats: as if—to use a Homeric simile—the late Henry Clay Frick were quoting the Beatitudes at a directors' meeting. The quality of Mr. Jones' what shall I say—sensibility?—I forbear to phrase, and leave it to the reader by quoting sonnet V entire:

> Go feed your brain on bitterness, feed it full,
> Give wormwood to your heart, and, fold on fold,
> Bid the snake, custom curl its treacherous gold
> About the secret places of your skull.
> It is therefore we are leaders, we who are dull
> But eminent. Our shining names are told,
> Our notable acts, our virtues are enrolled
> In *Who's Who in America* for you to cull.
>
> But do not meet meanwhile with your own ghost
> Who died before the god, Success, was born,
> For he will greet you with such wild surmise
> Flushing his cheeks and startling in his eyes
> As will revive the ambition, the pain, the lost
> Sweet passion and the beautiful young scorn.

Mr. Laurence Whistler, in his third volume, *The Emperor Heart*, comes highly recommended, by the present poet-laureate, Mr. John Masefield, for whom these verses are "unlike the writing of any other" and for whom Mr. Whistler's "thought is occupied with beauty." That is a pleasant subject to be occupied with, especially if one can write it up differently from anybody else. But I have a distinct impression gleaned from more than casual study of this little book, that Mr. Whistler's beauty is a little more local, in time and place, than Mr. Masefield's phrase would seem to allow it to be. The beauty seems to me to be pre-War English Georgian and to exist in terms of notations of the pretty park which is rural England, the corn, the wind, the spring, and the sheep, to say nothing of the distant manor house, nicely indicated but not quite ever reduced to any special rhythm or imagery that we have not seen before. But the evil times have marked Mr. Whistler: there is here and there a taint of the wicked metaphysical style:

> O put my arms about the vernal waist
> And close my eyes upon the immortal womb.

> Rest, rest, distracted frame, against the core
> Of all this darkening love that is your home—

But I should not want anybody to think that Mr. Whistler is always so uncomfortable:

> I went out in the gusty dark
> To see how that long corpse would look,
> But had not thought the moon was whirling
> Mottled-white like a new shilling—

The up-to-date note is struck here by the moon, but the rest is easy and reassuring. It is probably not necessary to exhibit another infidelity to beauty, the short poem "The Sepulchre," which acknowledges the existence of the later Yeats.

In *Darkling Plain* Miss Sara Bard Field brings us some of the enthusiasm and exuberant metaphor that persons like myself, ignorant of the Far West, usually associate with that fabulous region. But first of all in a "Note to Fellow Marxists" she warns them not to reach too deeply into the true doctrine in their verse, lest the very depth of emotion stirred by the Cause make for bad poetry. Miss Field reports a theory, passed on to her by Mr. John Cowper Powys, which she summarizes: "If composition takes place on the first and highest [plane], it will be superficial; if on the third and lowest, it will be self-involved. If, however, the intensity of the lowest stratum meets the detachment of the highest on a middle plane, a poem may be born." I do not know whether Mr. Powys is responsible for the imagery here, but it is a kind of poem itself, for the idea of a poem being born seems to me very nice. Mr. Powys gave Miss Field the theory in response to a poem that she had sent him, a poem "about an agonizing, pivotal, personal experience." I do not know whether any of the poems in this book are like that, and while I should not like to think Miss Field "superficial," the high, sustained soprano of her performance indicates constant occupation of the "first and highest" plane; or is the highest plane still higher? Or do I misunderstand the theory? Here are some lines to Elinor Wylie:

> Bright loveliness like cloisonné enamel
> Concealed a silver purpose so austere,
> So spherical of vision it could trammel

> Its fair, ephemeral coverture to clear
> Unhampered way for art's proud equipages
> To roll beyond her hour and bear her thought,
> Yet in those regal gifts despatched to ages
> Her beauty, ashes now, is also caught.

Miss Field invites constant rereading, and I am sure that her constant reader will agree with me that what she writes could hardly be better done.

Mr. C. F. MacIntyre is resourceful, and his book brings together intelligently but, I think, not for any strong purpose of his own, certain influences that were fashionable in the last decade. I do not mean that these influences are not still good—we shall see that Mr. Blackmur uses them to great advantage—yet it is plain that Mr. MacIntyre's facility is so omnivorous that he can take in Crane, Pound, Cummings, Eliot, and Ransom, and give them all back before he has discovered their relation to an intention of his own. There is not a poem in this volume that is quite all bad; but there is none entirely good. Mr. MacIntyre's first difficulty seems to me to exist for him prior to any considerations of style and prosody: his mind is stocked with phrases from the past and they get in his way. The ending of the poem, "For My Sister," which seems to be his most successful piece of composition, is ruined by an echo from one of Shakespeare's sonnets:

> She lives now, white in my mind, in a garland of leaves,
> quick yet as dawn pitched up by the moon's thin horn:
> a hill-top wisp not time's fell whip can tame,
> the wraith of my sister who was never born.

It profits Mr. MacIntyre but little to change "hand" to "whip": the insistence of the echo kept him from completing the image of the "wisp," and the line becomes further muddled by "tame," which is obviously there as a rhyme, remotely delayed, for "flame" and "name," six or seven lines back; but the rhyme being free and "organic," the need for it was not compelling, since there is no pattern to be completed.

It is this habit of using a phrase for its own sake, whether his own or somebody else's, that tends to make all of Mr. MacIntyre's poems sound alike—in spite of the frequent brilliant lines. Put into terms of immediate effect, the fault may be seen as one of composition; but more fundamentally the defect is a central one. There is seldom a reason why these poems should not be either longer or shorter than they are. The interesting "Remanded"—interesting in spite of the "influence" behind it, an influence that dominates the poem not merely in certain rhythms but even in the very syntax—would certainly be better for the absence of the last stanza; but Mr. MacIntyre was evidently overwhelmed by one of his least pertinent images—

> ... and the roots
> call the pink-nippled buds home for a nap—

and he wrote an eight-line stanza in order to use it. But in spite of this very distinct fault—and it is a fault of a somewhat prodigal gift for language—Mr. MacIntyre ought to be in his next book one of the good poets of the 'thirties if he can define for himself a little better what he wants to do.

If Mr. MacIntyre's trouble is a certain bewilderment amid so many phases of the period style of his elders, Mr. Lawrence Lee has, up to the present volume *Monticello and Other Poems*, paid too little attention to the innovations in language made by his immediate predecessors. I should not suggest that these innovations are valuable in themselves. Mr. Yeats, since about 1910, has made for himself a new poetic speech, but apart from what he conveys with it—if it were possible to consider it apart—his style is very close to some ideal of ordinary, educated speech: his immense originality consists in the peculiar kind of meaning, in the special vision of the world, different from any other, that this "ordinary" language is made to create. That is one way of making innovations of language in poetry. In Mr. Lee's new book there are still traces of his earlier manner, and I select at random this beginning of a sonnet called "Days Like Buttercups":

> Hardly the grass has come and they are there,
> Suddenly shaking yellow in the rain,
> Starring the green earth and the rain-washed air
> Like gathered dreams of childhood sprung again.

This is merely inoffensive, and it is not, as it is supposed by our popular critics, the central tradition of style. It is definitely a period style, 1900 to 1914. But throughout the book one finds moments of another sort of style, and doubtless Mr. Lee in his next book will tune his whole style to them, and not leave them scattered and almost accidental:

> The wind filled all dark outside with cold sound
> And rattled the windows of our house.

And this, from the title-poem:

> We shall not have from seasons peace, nor know
> Comfort in red leaves shaking.

I do not know whether Mr. Lee wrote these two passages with difficulty, but I surmise that a style based upon the very special rhythm and vowel sounds would give him or any other poet a hard time. Most of Mr. Lee's work is too easy for him, and it is my guess that greater technical stringency would lead him to important discoveries in sensibility and thought.

Miss Louise Bogan has published three books, and with each book she has been getting a little better, until now, in the three or four best poems of *The Sleeping Fury*, she has no superior within her purpose and range: among the women poets of our time she has a single peer, Miss Léonie Adams. Neither Miss Bogan nor Miss Adams will ever have the popular following of Miss Millay or even of the late Elinor Wylie. I do not mean to detract from these latter poets; they are technically proficient, they are serious, and they deserve their reputations. Miss Bogan and Miss Adams deserve still greater reputations, but they will not get them in our time because they are "purer" poets than Miss Millay and Mrs. Wylie. They are purer because their work is less involved in the moral and stylistic fashions of the age, and they efface themselves; whereas Miss Millay never lets us forget her "advanced" point of view, nor Mrs. Wylie her interesting personality.

This refusal to take advantage of the traditional privilege of her sex must in part explain Miss Bogan's small production and the concentrated attention that she gives to the detail of her work. Women,

I suppose, are fastidious, but many women poets are fastidious in their verse only as a way of being finical about themselves. But Miss Bogan is a craftsman in the masculine mode.

In addition to distinguished diction and a fine ear for the phrase-rhythm she has mastered a prosody that permits her to get the greatest effect out of the slightest variation of stress.

> In the cold heart, as on a page,
> Spell out the gentle syllable
> That puts short limit to your rage
> And curdles the straight fire of hell,
> Compassing all, so all is well.

There is nothing flashy about it; it is finely modulated; and I think one needs only to contrast Miss Bogan's control of her imagery in this stanza, the toning down of the metaphor to the simple last line, with the metaphorical juggernaut to which Miss Field's muse has tied herself, to see the fundamental difference between mastery of an artistic medium and mere undisciplined talent. Miss Bogan reaches the height of her talent in "Henceforth, from the Mind," surely one of the finest lyrics of our time. The "idea" of the poem is the gradual fading away of earthly joy upon the approach of age—one of the stock themes of English poetry; and Miss Bogan presents it with all the freshness of an Elizabethan lyricist. I quote the two last stanzas:

> Henceforth, from the shell,
> Wherein you heard, and wondered
> At oceans like a bell
> So far from ocean sundered—
> A smothered sound that sleeps
> Long lost within lost deeps,
> Will chime you change and hours,
> The shadow of increase,
> Will sound you flowers
> Born under troubled peace—
> Henceforth, henceforth
> Will echo sea and earth.

This poem represents the best phase of Miss Bogan's work: it goes back to an early piece that has been neglected by readers and reviewers alike—"The Mark"—and these two poems would alone entitle Miss Bogan to the consideration of the coming age.

But there is an unsatisfactory side to Miss Bogan's verse, and it may be briefly indicated by pointing out that the peculiar merits of "The Mark" and "Henceforth, from the Mind" seem to lie in a strict observance of certain limitations: in these poems and of course in others, Miss Bogan is impersonal and dramatic. In "The Sleeping Fury" she is philosophical and divinatory; in "Hypocrite Swift" she merely adumbrates an obscure dramatic situation in a half lyrical, half eighteenth-century, satirical style. Neither of these poems is successful, and the failure can be traced to all levels of the performances; for example, to the prosody, which has little relation to the development of the matter and which merely offers us a few clever local effects.

I have postponed consideration of Mr. Blackmur to the last, because with the publication of *From Jordan's Delight* we may see for the first time the capacity and range of one of the best poets of our time. It is to be expected from the critical conscience that Mr. Blackmur applies to his contemporaries, that he should exercise it upon himself. He is no longer, I suppose, a "young writer," yet surely some of these poems were written years ago and perhaps rewritten many times before their inclusion here. Blackmur could have published a volume of verse ten years ago: I infer that he has waited until he could offer a performance that meets the severe standards that he has demanded of others, in *The Double Agent*, which is the best technical criticism of poetry since *The Sacred Wood*.

Although Mr. Blackmur has been influenced by Stevens and Eliot, and even by Cummings and Hart Crane, his style is in no sense a period style, and is definitely his own. Echoes of his contemporaries appear chiefly in poems that are otherwise his least interesting work. The two impressive series of poems, "From Jordan's Delight" and "Sea Island Miscellany," contain none of these impurities, or if they do, they have been used so well that they are not easily detected. More positively Mr. Blackmur's style invites the technical criticism of which he has been so distinguished a practitioner: he is a poet with a high sense of form, and a considerable achievement of form spares us the speculative task of "obscure metaphysical reflection."

In the excellent piece called "The Spear," which is poem III of a series entitled "Dedications," there is a passage that I quote both for its substance, which is a kind of artistic credo, and for its style:

> Leave me my Odyssey,
> the living soul's hyperbole,
> peril in which to hide,
> peace for my naked eyes.
> O let my heart
> that spurns satieties
> be living hooked from the fresh flood
> but let my soul rehearse
> without benefit or curse
> of a saviour's blood
> its difficult and dangerous art.

Earlier in the poem there is the statement, "Salvation is a salmon speared,/the ancient Fisher cried." The spear of salvation may wait until death, and meanwhile without benefit of a supernatural religion, or in terms of Mr. Blackmur's immediate problem as a poet, without benefit of a "ready-made mould" of ideas, a structure of inevitable reference, he will practice the art of poetry. As to the style of this passage, it is sufficient to remark here that several of the terms are replaceable. The "Odyssey" is possibly the adventure of the discoverer of experience, but as a term it is merely allusive, not a fixed reference. Likewise "soul" is interchangeable with *mind* or *imagination*—which appreciably lowers the intensity of "hyperbole," and, in the line "but let my soul rehearse," is too weak to inform the action of the verb. So, here in this brief creed of the poet, we are at a loss to know what the foundation of his procedure is: fortunately he offers us other evidence—in addition to his concrete achievement, which is the best evidence—of the integrity of his purposes.

The interesting sequence of four sonnets, called "Judas Priest," "discusses" the relation of the artist to experience: that relation is simply that of Judas to the Passion of our Lord. I quote sonnet III:

> Judas, not Pilate, had a wakened mind
> and knew what agony must come about;

while Pilate washed his hands of all mankind,
he saw necessity past Pilate's doubt.

So driven mad did he alone indict
the waste the terror the intolerable loss,
the near abyss of darkness in the light,
and made a live tree of a wooden cross.

Where then are we?—we lookers-on of art,
outsiders by tormented wilful choice,
condemned to image death in each live heart,
and kiss it so—and how shall we rejoice?
  But if men prophesy Gethsemane
  Regardless, there must some regard the tree.

I have not quoted this as an example of Blackmur's best work, but
rather as a focus of some of his limitations, which if clearly grasped
will illuminate the essential properties of the eight or ten distinguished poems in this volume. Although Blackmur, in sonnet IV,
addresses the Communists as "comrades of a simpler faith," and
thus places his conception of the artist not only against the background of the Passion but also in terms of a contemporary "cause,"
he nevertheless seems to insist upon the quite simple distinction
between action and observation as the basis of his work. The poet
is not an indifferent Pilate; he is the Judas who betrays, in the sense
of remaining aloof from, action.

As I shall indicate in a moment, observation is not the exact word
for Blackmur's conception of the rôle of the poet. I have used it in a
preliminary distinction, in order to make the comment that all such
distinctions, action versus contemplation, morals versus art, are in
themselves neither sound nor unsound: a poet who eschews the in-
culcation of moral precepts may nevertheless be a morally sound
poet, and a poet who exhorts, like Mr. John Holmes, may have little
or no moral value. The tests of the distinction as Blackmur apprehends it must be found in his best verse.

Before we proceed to that, I shall seem again a little ungrateful to
Mr. Blackmur in pointing out defects in the quoted sonnet similar
to those in "The Spear." The sonnet is Shakespearean in form: three
quatrains developing serially towards the synthesis of the couplet;
at the ninth line begins the "application" of the matter set forth in

the two first quatrains, so that we get—what Shakespeare seldom used—an octet followed by quatrain-and-couplet so arranged as to imitate the effect of a genuine sestet; the couplet is detached grammatically but because it must complete the sense of the inconclusive twelfth line, it forms with the third quatrain a unit. Altogether this is as nice a piece of sonnet technique as you will find in modern verse; and the versification seems to me excellent. But there is something unsatisfactory in its total effect, and I think we may get at the difficulty through a brief analysis of the use of the word "necessity" in line four, the whole of line eight, and the play upon "regardless" and "regard" in the last line.

Why did Judas see "necessity" instead of an image—which would have been Yeats' way of dramatizing the scene? Mr. Blackmur gives us an uninformed and unsupported abstraction—as he does in the first of these four sonnets: "that watch new *bloodshed* waste god's death again." The entire second quatrain accumulates a series of rhetorical anti-images towards a climax which is thus not prepared for: the antithesis of tree and cross cuts off one's attention from the "scene" of the octet and is, in effect, the beginning of a core of meaning that, because the sonnet-structure demands it, is suddenly dropped. In the fourteenth line "regardless" means something like "without looking," "without care for the qualities inherent in the situation"; "regard" thus means "look at for its particular qualities." But the shock of the paranomasia here also is the beginning of a new "meaning," for the precision of the word-play exists on the purely logical, and not on the imaginative and synthesizing, plane.

This has been a long way round to a simple statement—and I have taken the long way because Blackmur is a poet who raises the fundamental problems of his art; he cannot be fixed in a generalization without one's previously showing how one has arrived at it. That simple statement is: Blackmur writes from two different *points d'appui*, the one abstract, the other immediate and dramatic. We have looked at the detail of two of his abstractly motived poems, and the conclusion seems inevitable: that Mr. Blackmur takes the "idea" first, and tries second to reduce it to image, with the result that the images do not materialize out of the idea. Of course, a merely logical reversal of this method would not remedy the trouble; but to state it so, on the bare logical basis, is enough I think to indicate the kind of defect that renders unsound this phase of Blackmur's work. Blackmur as a critic is a master of ideas, but as a poet he is occasionally mastered by them. But this does not mean that the idea as such, as a critical analysis of the function of poetry in relation to action, is unsound; it is rather that the idea is not available to Blackmur on the level of poetry. And this limitation witnesses again the difficulty of our age in writing philosophical poetry—a poetry springing from an apprehension, however profound, of ideas.

The distinction that I have just labored will, I hope, cast into bright relief the perfection of achievement in the bulk of Blackmur's poetry. I cannot do better than to quote one of the perfect lyrics (it is number IX of "Sea Island Miscellany" and is entitled "Mirage"):

> The wind was in another country, and
> the day had gathered to its heart of noon
> the sum of silence, heat, and stricken time.
> Not a ripple spread. The sea mirrored
> perfectly all the nothing in the sky.
> We had to walk about to keep our eyes
> from seeing nothing, and our hearts from stopping
> at nothing. Then most suddenly we saw
> horizon on horizon lifting up
> out of the sea's edge a shining mountain
> sun-yellow and sea-green; against it surf
> flung spray and spume into the miles of sky.
> Somebody said mirage, and it was gone,
> but there I have been living ever since.

As an historical reference for the poem I suppose the word *symbolism* is enough to indicate the sensibility and technique. The "human situation" is clearer than Mallarmé would have made it; the landscape is a little more toned down than Rimbaud would have liked; but it is definitely a symbolist poem.

Although it seems to me perfect of its kind—examine the adjectives in the fourth from the last line and the use of "miles" in the next line—it is not quite typical of Blackmur's best: I have quoted it to establish the extreme limit of his sensibility and so to point out that, at his best, his poetry arrives at form in terms of the implicit relation of a sensuous complex to the inherent order of his mind. And this method is precisely the opposite of the abstract pro-

cedure that I have analyzed in "The Spear" and in the sonnet from
"Judas Priest." Number V of "Sea Island Miscellany" will show the
method that Blackmur uses in his most characteristic poems:

> One grey and foaming day
> I looked from my lee shore
> landwards and across the bay:
> my eyes grew small and sore.
>
> Low in the low sea-waves
> the coast-line sank from sight;
> the viewless, full sea-graves
> stood open like the night:
>
> (sea waters are most bare
> when darkness spreads her trawl,
> the sea-night winds her snare
> either for ship or soul).
>
> Once along this coast
> my fathers made their sail
> and were with all hands lost,
> outweathered in a gale.
>
> Now from long looking I
> have come on second sight,
> there where the lost shores lie
> the sea is breeding night.

As in these poems, so in the most interesting work in this book, Mr.
Blackmur's imagery is derived from the natural phenomena of an
island off the coast of Maine, Jordan's Delight: it is more than imagery derived, for Blackmur has made the sea into a leading symbol
of the treachery of nature which constantly challenges the moral
resources of civilized man. This conflict, conceived not abstractly
but dramatically, in terms of experience, is the substance of a poetry
as good as any produced in our age. At another time it may be proper
to connect it with a wider historical background, and to look into
its significance as a special quality of the romantic sensibility. It is
a poetry that combines the richness of perception and the apparent
abandonment to the flux of experience, usually found in the romantic poets, with high form and implicit intellectual order.

From the Southern Review (Summer, 1937)

Walt Whitman

Whitman, by Edgar Lee Masters. Charles Scribner's Sons, 1937.

BECAUSE THERE IS a sense in which Whitman is the most neglected of American poets, it is time no doubt that he were given some close scrutiny by American critics. I do not mean that he is no longer written about; there is a formidable bulk of commentary upon him year after year, a sort of writing around his life, his times, his relation to Emerson, his fictitious six children, his sexual nature, his last days at Camden. While I cannot qualify as a Whitman expert, I am sure that little literary criticism—if his followers will concede that such a thing exists—has ever been written about him as a poet apart from his rôle as prophet. Even Mr. Santayana, in the best estimate of Whitman ever written, was interested in his "philosophical" views, not in the poetry as a contribution to an art. The monumental work is, of course, the immense book by the Frenchman, Jean Catel; it contains the best analysis of the esthetic value of Whitman; but there is no reference to that work in the new biography by Mr. Edgar Lee Masters.

Whitman is suffering the neglect that usually follows the achievement of a great name in literature; he is unusually difficult to write about because his prestige is due almost entirely to semi-political and semi-religious enthusiasm. Mr. Masters himself sees that such a reputation rests upon infirm ground: "Whitman's vision of America is big if America is big. If America fails he fails; and the defects of his performance in that case become more evident. He was a prophet, and if not a true one he must stand on his utterance as poetry." If I know what Mr. Masters is talking about, he means that unless America achieves a fairly complete Whitmanian democracy, the judgment of events must be unfavorable to Whitman's reputation. Mr. Masters contends that Whitman is better than Browning and Tennyson even as a "literary poet," but the evidence that he brings forward to support his argument (which may or may not be valid) is simply a reassertion of the glory of Whitman's "national vision," accompanied by the false assertion that neither of the English poets had it. So far then as Whitman's future reputation lies in the hands of Mr. Masters, it may be said that he will have none; for although the cause of democracy may not yet be defeated with us, the cause of Whitman's "dear love of comrades" never had any chance, and the value of "his utterance as poetry" is a problem mysterious to Mr. Masters, who refers to it occasionally but cannot keep his mind on it.

This book is the most curiously muddled performance that it has been my duty to attend for about ten years. There is no question but that Whitman's defects were shared by many of his contemporaries, both here and in England: Tennyson particularly succumbed to the temptations of literal prediction of the future, a kind of political whooping-it-up in verse. It was a general defect of the nineteenth-century poets that they based much of their performance not upon reality—through which the incidental and sole kind of prophecy may be achieved, as it was by Dante—but upon propaganda. I should not insist that Mr. Masters accept my all too inadequate suggestion of the nature of this problem; but I do think that we are entitled to ask him to be aware of it in terms of his own. He is aware neither of this elementary question—elementary in any discussion of a poet like Whitman—nor of any other problem of literature whatsoever. Here is his summary of Whitman's philosophy:

> Whitman saw in nature, beneath all shows and appearances, spirit and creative thought. This was the only absolute substance. He kept saying that he saw this. Good and evil, the opposing forces of positive and negative, were as the waves of the ocean which are contained within its body. . . .

That is the quality of Mr. Masters' intellect, its quality at its best. It is a mind that reflects at the mere level of uncritical absorption all the libertarian ideas of the early Nineteenth Century: at that level the ideas are not the equipment of a critic, and the biographer of a poet must be a literary critic before he approaches the poet's life. It must be said that Mr. Masters tries valiantly, if incoherently, to present the unpleasant side of Whitman's character, nor does he spare him criticism of his limitations—as he conceives one of them, for example, in the following passage:

> He saw that the objection to the nude, and shame of the body were of Asiatic origin, without laying his hands directly upon the Bible as the source in American life of those preposterous prejudices. . . . When giving Jesus the great preëminence [over Socrates] that he did he lagged behind Elizabeth Cady Stanton, an American product of the same times as those which produced Whitman.

It is a curious fact that a book as good as *Spoon River Anthology* should have been written by the village atheist.

From *Poetry* (September, 1937)

Yeats's Last Friendship

Letters on Poetry from W. B. Yeats to Dorothy Wellesley. Oxford University Press, 1940.

I SUPPOSE THAT Dorothy Wellesley is Yeats's Trelawny: she saw a great deal of him from 1935 to the end of his life: she was even present when he died, and followed the body to the grave. But the analogy cannot be pressed too far; and I think we may be simply grateful that Yeats in the last three years had a friend who had not known him before and who could thus see this final phase with unprejudiced eyes. Lady Gerald does more than that: we are likely to underestimate the tact and intelligence of her friendship with Yeats, and to miss some of her value for him, because Yeats himself overestimated her poetry (as it seems to us now). We feel that in view of what has been happening in Anglo-American poetry in the past decade, Yeats might have given his confidence to a somewhat more "contemporary" person, not to a merely charming woman.

But I think this point of view is wrong. Lady Gerald—as Dorothy Wellesley—has edited these letters with a distinct awareness of two very important features of Yeats's last years. The commentary with which she fills out the gaps in the correspondence, and I should think even the selections from her own letters, point constantly to the image of the old poet who not only had a new burst of poetic energy but extended his technical resources and, ill most of the time, wrote some of his greatest poems. (A "charming woman" would have been charmed and flattered by Yeats's attention, but here there is none of the gross effect of flattery: Lady Gerald has a clarity and moderation of judgment that appear in many observations: "Sex, Philosophy and the Occult preoccupy him. He strangely intermingles all three. The old masters, the dead accepted poets about which I much desire his opinion, appear to weary him." Again: ". . . His lack of observation concerning natural beauty was almost an obsession, and it . . . dims most poems of his concerned with Nature." Not criticism but direct and valuable observation.)

And then there is his revival of interest in "popular poetry," through broadsides printed by the Cuala Press, which in some fashion yet to be explored curiously parallels the rise of social consciousness in the younger English poets. Yeats was fully conscious of the difference between himself and these young men: he wanted poems that would be sung, or at least repeated until they had been severed from their authors. "Think like a wise man, but express yourself like the common people," he says again and again—very nearly the contrary of the procedure of the younger men, who have tried to think *with* the "common people" in complicated styles. Yeats, in his way, was perfectly aware of his situation in his time, and this correspondence will make it dangerous for later writers to assume that he had made a "retreat" away from what is sometimes mystically referred to as the "center of the age." The question may in the end come to the decision of history: whether the "people" in mass societies can express themselves, and the poet himself, through their language at all; whether expression will not be violence, through unrepresentative leaders; but about this nobody knows anything.

From *The New Republic* (November 25, 1940)

The Last Omnibus

Poems, 1930–1940, by Horace Gregory. Harcourt, Brace, 1941.
50 Poems, by E. E. Cummings. Duell, Sloan, and Pearce, 1941.
Cantos LII–LXXI, by Ezra Pound. New Directions, 1940.
Five Young American Poets: An Anthology. New Directions, 1941.

THERE OUGHT to be a law against omnibus reviews and perhaps even against reviewing as many as two books together unless it is obvious that they ought to go together; and although I do not know who should decide that a connection exists, it ought not to be left to the penetration of the reviewer. There is no doubt some connection between Grimm's law and the latest patriotic homily by Mr. Henry Luce, but I do not know who could take the responsibility for it. The field of references supplied by a miscellany of last month's books is likely to have as much critical value as the matrix of military analogy through which Uncle Toby ordered his experience; and it has very little chance of being half so entertaining. In a review that includes Horace Gregory, Ezra Pound, E. E. Cummings, to say nothing of the Five Young Poets, the best that anybody can hope to do is to take each of them up in turn as a stick to beat the others over the head with.

We could easily begin by beating Horace Gregory over the head with a stick called Ezra Pound. (I confess that my heart isn't in it, but what else can I do? It is one of our most recent conventions, practiced with varying degrees of brutality, vanity, and skill, by the "younger men," e.g., Jarrell and Levin; and if there is anything better calculated to attract attention than the bad manners of a young man, it is the bad manners of an old man; by which rule I may expect to be fifteen times as brutal, vain, and skillful, as the young, being fifteen years older.) We have our analogy of the stick, which will be our critical approach throughout, and it will fortunately keep us from having to say anything about the people we beat with it.

Horace Gregory: one of the best poets of his generation in the United States; has never got his due; publishes too much, the too much in this book being most of the pieces written since *Chorus for Survival*; has a fine ear—or rather, I suspect, had it, unless the collapse of "The Postman's Bell Is Answered Everywhere," a recent poem, is only temporary. In this poem the loose rhythms are accompanied by a kind of willed documentation, in which there is little clean observation or energy of metaphor. There was a good deal of this sort of thing in the early poems: it came, I suspect, from the self-imposed obligation to uphold a social point of view which I have never been able to feel was congenial to Gregory. I mean congenial to him as a poet. For there are two things that he does supremely well and I do not know whether anybody has discussed them: elegy and nostalgia, and the two are constantly interwoven of the materials of his boyhood and ancestry. The shocked awareness that "industrial America" compromises the innocence of these emotions becomes articulated in something that may be roughly described as Marxism; hence the flat passages of social documentation which have an air of deliberate self-torture. It is as if the poet were saying, "I hate this, and if it could be corrected (by Marxism) I might recover the innocence of my childhood." This is perfectly serious, and is one of the historic situations of poets; for however complex a poet's nerves may be, his "ideology" tends to gross simplification. Our tradition of more than a century of blaming society for lost innocence makes us oscillate between nostalgia on the one hand and indictment on the other; but when Gregory gets out of this trap he writes some of the best poetry of the time. I would cite a great deal of *No Retreat* and most of *Chorus for Survival*, particularly number 15 of the latter. It is now time for somebody to undertake a close enquiry into this poet, to see what he adds up to.

What I have to say about Pound is going to be perfunctory: the new Cantos leave me very, very cold; and short of a roundabout survey of all the Cantos, the less said the better. Respect for Mr. Pound, were there enough space, could easily lead to the collection of small garlands, even from the new book; there are many beautiful passages lying limp on the sand. Some reviewers have remarked that Pound has no prosody in the new Cantos. I think this is a mistake: he has exactly the same prosody that he had in Canto I. The difference is in the subject-matter. In the first thirty we were able to attribute structure to the verse because we felt a certain historical unity in the material: there is for us something like a direct line from Homeric Greece through the Italian Renaissance to modern Europe; but between John Adams and the agrarian emperors of China there is only a community of economic abstraction, which Major Douglas alone understands today, and of high courtesy, which Mr. Pound evidently despairs of reviving.

If Cummings was as good as most people said he was fifteen years ago, he couldn't be as bad now as the neglect of *50 Poems* by the reviewers makes him out to be. If Cummings is now taking the penalty of a chichi reputation in the twenties, there is every reason to believe that the people who built him up in that special way ought to suffer it with him; but of course they will not. Nobody in those days was stronger for Cummings than Edmund Wilson, who was tireless in pointing out to us every novelty that Cummings produced. Have Cummings' defenders departed because he no longer produces novelties? Scattered poems in all his books, the greater portion of *and*, and three or four poems in the new book are among the best work of our time. Of these last, poem 34 ("my father moved through dooms of love") is the most moving and brilliant, and it is likely to be missed by readers who are certain that in the other new poems Cummings is doing his old typographical act as a routine and is producing nothing "new." This act seems to me to be as new as it ever was, and in itself as tiresome; but neither better nor worse.

In *Five Young American Poets* New Directions begins an annual anthology for poets who have not published a book and who, in the present state of commercial publishing, might get less attention individually than they would as a group. It is a good plan, but if Mr. Laughlin feels that he must put out five young poets every year, his standards will begin to sink somewhere around the third year: I suggest occasional rather than annual publication. Here each poet has forty pages, complete with photograph, holograph fragment, and self-written introduction. Mr. Jarrell's introduction is easily the best, for what one would expect actually happens: when he discusses himself the savagery of the wit which he turns upon others mellows a little, and we see something of the genuine critical power that he will no doubt develop further. Mr. Berryman's self-scrutiny is intelligent but unnecessary; it comes to the conclusion that a poem cannot be paraphrased. Mr. O'Donnell sets up a high traditional standard before which he feels a modesty that does not wholly convince me. I cannot remember what Mr. Moses says. And Miss Barnard sets out to say nothing and, with a great deal of propriety, succeeds.

I must confess that the great hopes I had for this anthology have been a little disappointed. There is a great deal of talent here, and it may mature in the next few years. At present even Jarrell and Berryman, the most brilliant of the five, do not quite come off. It is not that they still exhibit their influences: Eliot still shows traces of his. As to Jarrell, the main influence is Auden—which is neither here nor there; but it is very much to the point that he seems to be so afraid of writing an organized accentual-syllabic line that he gives the impression of roughening the metre without an eye to any definite effect. The result is frequently merely an accentual line which can be scanned but not read. There is something casual and at the same time, indirectly, a little pretentious about the effect. Nevertheless, so far as I can see, Jarrell is the best we have to offer as a white hope for poetry in his generation. He has written three or four poems that can compete without embarrassment with the best of our time.

At a glance Berryman looks still better, and he may actually be better; though I doubt it. In terms of what he is doing he has considerably more control than Jarrell, but it is possible that the conrol is premature. For example, too many of his poems go off into the fixed direction of the meditative convention of Yeats: at his comparatively early age he seems to have got set in the tone of pronouncement and prophecy, with the result that his powers of observation are used chiefly for incidental shock. Yet his line has more firmness and structure than Jarrell's, and there is a sense in which he is more mature: he is not afraid to commit himself to systematic and even solemn elaborations of metaphor. So in his way he is bolder than

Jarrell, line by line, but within a structural timidity of feeling which I believe comes of his too great reliance upon Yeats.

These men would be good poets anywhere. (How many poets, in any ultimate sense, "come off"?) O'Donnell's poetry has puzzled me for some years. He has been almost wholly successful in frustrating himself with certain influences (chiefly Ransom) that have come his way. I think the main trouble with O'Donnell is that his poems are less structures of feeling and image than public performances, of which "Commencement Oration" is typical. He has succumbed even more completely than Berryman to the tone and convention of "In Memory of Major Robert Gregory." But on the credit side it must be said that his mimicry has a certain innocent quality, which may mean that he lacks self-consciousness and that he may develop genuine power when he matures. There is no doubt about his gift for language.

I can see Mr. Moses' virtues, but after reading his section three times, I could not remember an individual poem, and I decided that his virtues were not interesting. I think Miss Barnard might be more interesting if she applied the same finical anxiety to the development of a prosody that she applies now to avoiding one.

From *Partisan Review* (May–June, 1941)

W. H. Auden

The Double Man, by W. H. Auden. Random House, 1941.

THE OLDER I get the less I feel like writing about the poetry of my contemporaries, except by way of excerpt and generalization; I am so envious of their successes and so impatient of their failures that I cannot fool even myself with the pretense of impartiality. Envy and impatience make a hard dilemma but envy and gloating would make an easy one. I cannot gloat over the failures; I want poetry to be good; and when it is very good I envy it. I am plagued by this unhappy state when I go through Auden's *The Double Man;* I can see in it a great deal that is brilliant and entertaining, and in the sonnets much that is brilliant and moving; but in passage after passage the main poem, "New Year Letter," slides off into a fast one—the "hand is quicker than the eye" of parlor magic—or in places it dissolves into the annotations, of which there are 87 pages to 55 of poetic text. And the sonnet sequence, called "The Quest," ought to be much better—how much I do not know, but at least as good as the sonnets in Auden's first book or those in *Journey to a War;* and I think they would have been that good had he put in about fifteen more minutes on each sonnet, which would have come to a total of five hours for the sequence: not much as poets count time.

Anything else that I can say about this book will be detail for what I have just said. At the end of Part II of "New Year Letter" Auden brings in "the devil who controls / The moral asymmetric souls," and after telling us that "He cannot always fool us thrice" with lies but will give us half-truths that we can "synthesize," he describes the role of the double man:

> So, hidden in this hocus-pocus,
> There lies the gift of double focus,
> The magic lamp which looks so dull
> And utterly impractical
> Yet, if Aladdin use it right,
> Can be a sesame to light.

Here the hand is quicker than the eye; but Auden himself reveals the trick in his note to the passage. The asymmetric souls are the lazy romantics who refuse, says Auden, to recognize a paradox when they meet one; then he goes on in the next note to tell us that the devil is the father of poetry, "for poetry might be defined as the clear expression of mixed feelings." Very good; and the notes are more illuminating than the verse text because they are direct and clear. The metaphorical expression of the idea in the verse text only muddles it up; it is, in fact, an example of the sort of romanticism which it purports to expose. We may get at it this way:

The figure of Aladdin's lamp is brought in to resolve the paradox; rub it and we get light. The figure is further complicated by introducing from another Arabian Night the word "sesame" (the name of a grain) which, spoken, opens up the robbers' cave. So we get an equivalence: the wonders of the cave are light, and light is a stock symbol (that's nothing against it) for truth. Now in this casual but actually sophisticated and complex metaphor the main idea of conflict, of paradox, or, in terms of the knowing mind, of double focus which must see and, in terms of poetry, must dramatize, is shunted off and lost altogether. The subject of this passage is paradox; it is presented monistically in a single image of light. So the real paradox here is one which I believe Auden was not aware of: the contradiction between his idea and the metaphor for it.

Throughout the poem there is a certain inadequacy of his command over metaphor which makes his elaborate notes necessary or at any rate illuminating. His poetic language leaves something out; it would be better to say that it can't get it all in. And when a poet can't get it all in, when his language is too simple for his subject, he is ignoring some of it; and I think that Auden would agree that such a poet is the "impatient romantic" who ignores part of a conflict after being aware of the whole. (Not the "lazy romantic" who is not aware in the first place.) Or we may put the matter thus: in terms of Auden's views of the poet, he is a non-romantic man who becomes a romantic poet.

The question is in the long run quite simple. If you will look at the greater poems of Yeats—the Byzantium poems or the Crazy Jane series—you will see the same double focus on irreconcilable opposites. But the opposition is conveyed in a structure of metaphor which retains the conflict:

> That dolphin-torn, that gong-tormented sea

and many other examples, one of them being the entire poem from which this line is quoted. Auden has a complex, even a very rich mind; yet his passion for autobiography brings him back always to the question: What does it mean to me? Perhaps he will not be able to tell us fully what it means to him until he no longer asks the question. Or maybe until he asks this question: What does it mean?

From *Accent* (Winter, 1942)

New Poems: 1942

New Poems: 1942. An Anthology of British and American Verse, edited by
Oscar Williams. Peter Pauper Press, 1942.

THE SECOND of Mr. Williams's anthologies may be a little bet-
ter than the first, published last year as New Poems: 1940, though
I cannot find anything in the new one that strikes me as quite up to
Empson's "Missing Dates," which seems to me a poem in a lifetime.
But comparison of the two collections is not profitable. What, rather,
is the merit of this book, and what purpose does it serve? Does it
make current enough good poetry to justify it? I think that it does.
I do not like anthologies, but I like anthologies better than nothing.
For this is an age in which they are peculiarly valuable: books by
young poets, and some books by older poets, do not sell. It is a difficulty easy to take advantage of, and we must be suspicious of new
anthologists. Last year I was suspicious of Mr. Williams. Now I am
convinced of his disinterested purposes, as I think anyone must be
who has read his Introduction to New Poems: 1942.

It is something at any rate to have given us, in the midst of the
greatest war, eight or ten very fine poems. "At the Grave of Henry
James" is the best Auden, though it is a little stuffed in places. Jarrell's "90 North" and Shapiro's "Scyros" ought to prove to the most
obdurate that we have at least two young poets—both are under
thirty—who could have more than held their own back in the twenties, which are now referred to as the good old days of poetry. Blackmur's "Missa Vocis" is very Yeatsian, more than it needs to be, but it
remains a very good poem. I miss here Warren's "Terror," which must
have been available—it is Warren's best poem—yet the four pieces
representing this poet are among his best and ought to remind us of

the injustice which has kept his reputation somewhat private. Miss Rukeyser's "Ajanta," a poem based upon a Hindu myth, I admire greatly: it has a close texture and controlled rhythms; and the poetry is all *in* the poem, not three-fourths of it participating merely by allusion to some field of Miss Rukeyser's sympathies, like the proletariat or airplanes. (I confess that Miss Rukeyser's poetry has hitherto bored me.) W. R. Rodgers's "End of a World" is interesting, but beyond the fact that it is a war poem I do not know what it is; I like it line by line, but having read it four times without being able to remember anything in it, I begin to suspect that the fault is not wholly mine.

The poems by Jarrell, Shapiro, and Rodgers are all war poems. There are other war poems which I shall not cite, but I shall cite two more, making four (counting Rodgers out), very brilliant examples of war verse. One of the best poems of this war was written in 1932, "The Return," by John Peale Bishop; it has been published many times, but I think that Mr. Williams is right in claiming it as new. It is one of the leading poems of our time. Horace Gregory's "Voices of Heroes" has a very good chance to survive as the best poem by an American which has been directly prompted by this war. It is nonsense to complain that we are not getting good war poetry. Unless my memory betrays me, it is better than the poetry of the last war. Its range is greater; it takes in more of the total human experience; there is now much less of think-only-this-of-me, and a more intelligent awareness that war poetry ought to be poetry, not merely complaint.

Not all the verse in this book is good, or even good enough to be in it; much of it is the price we've had to pay for Auden's best, which, imitated, sounds like his worst. I have singled out some of the good things in order to correct a balance in favor of the poets, who are good enough today for any age. In times of peace the industrialists, the bankers, and the statesmen get credit for "civilization"; in time of war the imaginative writer gets credit for its fall. This hollow and possibly ominous nonsense will prevail for a while, but unless Mr. Williams wished to convict Mr. MacLeish of special pleading in connection with the Proust-caused-the-fall-of-France theory, I can see no reason for the presence of MacLeish's "The

Spanish Dead" in this book. It is the worst poem in it; it is hortatory, insipid, and unfinished. Let us, in kindness to MacLeish, hold the belief that although the poets are not irresponsible, his own verse has gone sour for a while.

There is good new work by Stevens (not his best), by Spender and Thomas and Spencer, but not, alas, by Schwartz and MacNeice. Three new women poets will bear watching: Jean Garrigue, Gene Derwood, and Ruth Herschberger. I hope that Mr. Williams will do this job again.

From The Nation (June 13, 1942)

Karl Shapiro

Person, Place and Thing, by Karl Jay Shapiro. Reynal & Hitchcock, 1942.

DEAR SHAPIRO:
You will understand that I have doubted the propriety of addressing to you as a letter this review of your first book of verse, *Person, Place and Thing*; for I have not met you. Although I am well-acquainted among men of my age, the literary generations come on so fast that I cannot even assume that you know who I am. No matter. War has its own way of making us shift our glance, yours, perhaps, as well as mine. I cannot be sure that I should have been able, in the ungenerous revery into which men fall in their first middle-age, to read your poems—read them, I mean, with the selfless attention which they demand—but for the coming of the war; and if I may surmise your interests and loyalties, I suspect that you would have felt, when you left for Australia last year, as you may feel now, a certain indifference towards any attention from me. It has been so since there have been conscious literatures. These barriers I have decided to ignore, for two reasons.

First, your poetry has moved me profoundly, and I cannot at this early stage of my acquaintance with it have the certainty of judgment which ought to inform a conventional review. Secondly, you are the first poet, much younger than myself, of whom I feel a steady and disturbing envy.

The two reasons are intimately related. Your poetry moves me because it has, for the first time since T. S. Eliot's arrival more than twenty-five years ago, that final honesty which is rare, unpleasant, and indispensable in a poet of our time. I envy you because, having striven for this quality, I have failed; I have never, in any poem, been able *to get it all down*. You very nearly do get it all down, at moments wholly. I address you from a past remotely different from yours, from a radically different conception of the history and destiny of this common country of ours; yet if you will allow me the sentiment, the common humanity of poets is not founded in sympathy of views or of politics, but in that special savagery of attack which they must acknowledge across all barriers, as I wish at this moment to acknowledge it in your poems.

In this letter there is no place for criticism; of that you will get enough elsewhere, and some of it may not please you. You will be told that you have too much of Auden, even a little of Crane, and here and there a prim phrase (but never a passage) that Marianne Moore might have written. You will also be told that you are too clever, that your magnificent powers of invention often overreach their object. Let me put this in psychological or even moral terms. You have a Baudelairean disgust; yet you sometimes elaborate your disgust into mere convention, as in "The Fly," where the conceit wears itself out as badly as any of Cleveland's or Cowley's. For honesty itself has its own excesses, which are made manifest in the merely personal anger that I seem to detect in poems like "Washington Cathedral," "Alexandria," "Waitress," and in scattered lines. Here there is a loss of power, a rhetorical vertigo, which reveals the generous young man, but not the poet. Crane used to shout, "We have got to slap *all* humanity in the face!" It is not easy; it is much easier to slap the nearest faces.

May I list here certain poems that for me are already placed in the best poetry of our time? I think first of "The Dome of Sunday," then of "Necropolis" and "Elegy for Two Banjos;" and close after these, "Scyros," "Love Poem," and "Travelogue for Exiles." In these poems there is a fine control of tone and an unpredictable rightness of observation which nobody else of your generation has achieved. And there is also great power. Are not these qualities enough? If it does not strike you as too old-fashioned, let me congratulate you, and hope that you will be among those who return.

From *Common Sense* (February, 1943)

Robert Lowell

Introduction to *Land of Unlikeness*, by Robert Lowell. Cummington Press, 1944.

THERE IS no other poetry today quite like this. T. S. Eliot's recent prediction that we should soon see a return to formal and even intricate metres and stanzas was coming true, before he made it, in the verse of Robert Lowell. Every poem in this book has a formal pattern, either the poet's own or one borrowed, as the stanza of "Satan's Confession" is borrowed from Drayton's "The Virginian Voyage," and adapted to a personal rhythm of the poet's own.

But this is not, I think, a mere love of external form. Lowell is consciously a Catholic poet, and it is possible to see a close connection between his style and the formal pattern. The style is bold and powerful, and the symbolic language often has the effect of being *willed*; for it is an intellectual style compounded of brilliant puns and shifts of tone; and the willed effect is strengthened by the formal stanzas, to which the language is forced to conform.

A close reader of these poems will be able to see two general types, or extremes which it is the problem of the poet to unite, but which I believe are not yet united: this is not a fault, it merely defines the kind of poet that Lowell, at this early stage, seems to be. On the one hand, the Christian symbolism is intellectualized and frequently given a savage satirical direction; it points to the disappearance of the Christian experience from the modern world, and stands, perhaps, for the poet's own effort to recover it. On the other hand, certain shorter poems, like "A Suicidal Nightmare" and "Death from Cancer," are richer in immediate experience than the explicitly religious poems; they are more dramatic, the references being personal and historical and the symbolism less willed and explicit.

The history of poetry shows that good verse does not inevitably make its way; but unless, after the war, the small public for poetry shall exclude all except the democratic poets who enthusiastically greet the advent of the slave-society, Robert Lowell will have to be reckoned with. Christopher Dawson has shown in long historical perspective that material progress may mask social and spiritual decay. But the spiritual decay is not universal, and in a young man like Lowell, whether we like his Catholicism or not, there is at least a memory of the spiritual dignity of man, now sacrificed to mere secularization and a craving for mechanical order.

Alphabetical Listing of Poets Reviewed